RIG *for* HOME OWNERS

revised and updated by
Paul Moorhouse and David Thomas

10th edition

SHAC
Kingsbourne House
229-231 High Holborn
London WC1V 7DA
Tel 071 404 7447

CPAG
4th Floor
1-5 Bath Street
London EC1V 9PY
Tel 071 253 3406

© CPAG Ltd and SHAC, 1994

CPAG Ltd   ISBN 0 946744 58 0
SHAC   ISBN 0 948857 71 4

Cover artwork by Devious Designs (0742-755634)
Typeset by Nancy White (071-607 4510)
Printed by Blackmore Press (0747 853034)

CPAG

CPAG has been at the forefront of the fight against family poverty in Britain since its foundation as a national charity in 1965. Its specialist welfare rights team provides a national resource for benefits advisers, with the aim of ensuring that low-income families get the welfare benefits to which they are entitled. CPAG is also the leader in the field of welfare rights training.

Every year it publishes the widely-acclaimed *National Welfare Benefits Handbook*, the *Rights Guide to Non-Means-Tested Benefits* and the *Child Support Handbook*. Other publications include the *Council Tax Handbook, Fuel Rights Handbook, Debt Advice Handbook, CPAG's Housing Benefits and Council Tax Benefit Legislation* and a range of books on poverty and related issues.

The best way of keeping up-to-date with welfare rights and poverty issues is to join CPAG as a member. Members also support CPAG's work for a fairer future for low-income families and their children. For further details of CPAG's publications, training courses and membership schemes, please write to CPAG, 1-5 Bath Street, London EC1V 9PY.

David Thomas is CPAG's Legal Officer.

SHAC

SHAC opened in 1970 as London's first independent housing aid centre. Its work covers the whole range of housing problems, including homelessness, security of tenure, disrepair and mortgage arrears. Over the past 24 years, SHAC has given advice and help to over 150,000 households.

SHAC's publications and training courses draw on this direct advice-giving experience; it produces a range of advice booklets, publishes research into major housing issues and provides information and training for a wide range of voluntary and statutory organisations.

For further information about SHAC publications and training courses, contact the Promotions Dept at Kingsbourne House, 229-231 High Holborn, London WC1V 7DA.

Paul Moorhouse is SHAC's Housing Debt Worker.

ACKNOWLEDGEMENTS

The authors would like to thank Jim Gray for his work in incorporating coverage of the law in Scotland in this edition, and Jim McKenny, Lorraine Thompson, Rosemary Guest and Simon Lidster of the Inland Revenue for reading and checking the manuscript.

Thanks are also due to Linda Davies for producing the book, to Fran Newell for indexing it, and to Linda Davies, Peter Ridpath and Debbie Haynes for marketing and distributing it.

SHAC is also grateful to the London Borough Grants Scheme for agreeing to release Paul Moorhouse to work on this book.

This edition of the *Rights Guide for Home Owners* builds upon the valuable work of others who prepared the original text and its subsequent revisions. The original authors were Jo Tunnard and Clare Whately. Later editions were revised and updated by Janet Allbeson, Lorna Gordon, Ken Baublys, Beth Lakhani, Lorraine Thompson, Jan Luba, Simon Ennals, Sue Spaull, Derek McConnell and Jim McKenny.

Contents

Introduction	vii
1 Understanding your mortgage	**1**
How mortages work	1
Types of mortgages	3
Types of insurance policies	8
Types of lenders	10
Government help with your mortgage	12
2 How to increase your income: working full time	**14**
Family credit	14
Disability working allowance	19
Housing benefit	24
Council tax benefit	24
Education benefits	24
Health benefits	25
Social fund payments	26
Other benefits and grants	26
3 How to increase your income: not working full time	**27**
Income support	28
Income support and your mortgage interest	36
When you receive less than your full housing costs	37
How to pay unmet interest, mortgage capital or insurance premiums	44
Challenging decisions about your income support	47
Other related benefits	48
The social fund scheme	49
Other benefits	51
4 Council tax and council tax benefit	**52**
Council tax	52
Council tax benefit	55
5 Cutting your mortgage costs	**61**
Getting help and advice	62
If you have one mortgage	63
If you have two or more mortgages	67
Consumer Credit Act loans	70
Appeals to lenders	71

6 Dealing with arrears

How lenders reclaim a loan	72
How to keep your home	74
Clearing your mortgage arrears	79
Consumer Credit Act loans	83

7 Repairs and improvements

Grants from the local authority	85
Other help from local authorities	87
Applying for local authority grants	88
Grants from the Home Energy Efficiency Scheme	90
Loans from other sources	91
Responsibility for repairs if you are a leaseholder	94

8 Separation

Introduction	103
What to do in the short term	104
What to do in the long term	109
How to negotiate with your lender	115
Income after separation	116
Income tax for separated partners	121

9 If you lose your home

If your home is repossessed	127
If the sale price does not clear the debts	129
Mortgage rescue schemes	130
Buying another home	131
Shared ownership schemes	136
Rented accommodation	136
Homelessness and local authorities	138

Appendices

1	How to work out your mortgage repayments	141
2	How to calculate family credit	146
3	Income support rates until April 1995	148
4	Rules about savings and capital for income support, family credit, council tax benefit, housing benefit and disability working allowance	151
5	Specimen letters requesting a loan for repairs	154
6	Legal aid	156
7	Useful addresses	160
8	Financial statements – example	163
9	Useful publications	166

Index 167

Introduction

In Britain today many more people own their homes than rent them. The vast majority of 'homeowners', however, live in houses or flats which have mortgages or other loans secured on them. Between 1982 and 1993 the number of mortgages in England and Wales increased from 6,518,000 to 10,137,000.

This has been accompanied by a much greater increase in the number of people experiencing difficulties in keeping up with their mortgage payments. Over the same period, the number of mortgages more than six months in arrears increased from 32,890 (0.5 per cent of all mortgages) to 316,430 (3.12 per cent of all mortgages).

In 1982, 6,820 people had their homes repossessed by their mortgage lenders. By 1993, this had grown to 68,540. This total was down from the 1991 all-time record of over 75,000 repossessions but still represents an increase from roughly one in 1,000 mortgagors to nearly one in 150. Recently the figures have improved, with 15,040 repossessions in the first half of 1994 compared with 22,426 in the same period in 1993.

Recent research carried out for Shelter has shown a welcome decline over the year to March 1994 in the number of mortgages in arrears, but points out that there are still almost 268,000 households with long-term debts for whom 'the reality is that these families *do* continue to be at risk of losing their homes'.

Another serious problem, both for people who have lost their homes and for those seeking to avoid this, is the massive growth in negative equity – when people owe more on their home than it is worth. Research published by the Joseph Rowntree Foundation in December 1993 showed that one in four people who had bought houses since 1987 were in this situation. This not only means that people can lose their houses and still owe large sums of money, but it also narrows the options available to people trying to avoid having their homes repossessed.

This situation, which remains a serious crisis affecting the lives of a large proportion of Britain's population, has its roots in a number of factors. These include the crash in the property market, and the recession which has slashed household incomes, but these have been added to by a number of other problems:

- ☐ The decline in the value of benefits and the widening gap between the poorest households in Britain and the rest of the population has seriously reduced the effectiveness of welfare benefits as a safety net for homeowners on low incomes. In particular, the absence of any kind of benefit to meet the housing costs of owner-occupiers working more than 16 hours a week forces many people to choose between employment and keeping their home. In addition, the recent income support rules which in general terms limit the interest the Benefits Agency will pay to loans of £125,000, and prevent any interest being paid for a new or increased loan if you are already on income support, are likely to cause serious problems for many people.

- ☐ While the mortgage arrears crisis of the last five years has led many lenders to re-examine their policies, advisers still encounter far too many examples of a lack of sympathy, prejudice and even bureaucratic incompetence on the part of lenders, leading to people losing their homes.

- ☐ Similarly, the difficulties experienced by people trying to claim benefits have meant that homeowners often cannot obtain money which they are entitled to. The Benefits Agency estimates that £158 million per year of mortgage interest payments are dealt with incorrectly. The Money Advice Association believes this could mean nearly 100,000 households a year receive incorrect mortgage payments from the Benefits Agency. Many of these people risk losing their homes as a direct result.

These problems mean that in order to stand a chance of keeping their homes, homeowners hit by low incomes, redundancy, relationship breakdown, illness and other difficulties which can lead to mortgage arrears, need access to information about their rights and how to enforce them. Over nine editions, this *Guide* has a proven track record in providing the necessary facts and advice.

This edition contains information about your mortgage; about your rights to welfare benefits; and about your legal rights to keep your home. We have included information about the Child Support Act and its impact on the incomes of families following separation; the new Leasehold Reform Housing and Urban Regeneration Act and the new rights of leaseholders; and about your options if you are faced with negative equity.

The *Guide* explains the steps which can be taken to try to maintain mortgage payments and prevent the loss of your home. All too often, a small amount of arrears brought about by a drop in income, or an unexpected event like relationship breakdown, has been the start of a cycle which has led to homelessness. Yet this need not happen.

There are many steps which a family can take to maintain their mortgage repayments and thus keep their home. Borrowers and their advisers must consider the mortgage arrangements, the best use of welfare benefits and tax allowances, and aspects of property and family law, as well as the availability of alternative accommodation. Sadly, in our experience, lenders, solicitors and other advisers have not always had the necessary knowledge to advise families on the best way to keep their homes.

This *Guide* gives practical, step-by-step advice on how to cut mortgage costs, increase income and negotiate with lenders, the courts, Benefits Agency offices and local authorities. Because mortgage difficulties often arise when a relationship breaks down, we have given special attention to the problems faced by the single parent who is left with the children and threatened with loss of the home.

The *Guide* deals with the law as it applies in England, Wales and Scotland. The law and procedures are described as we understand them to be on 1 August 1994.

CHAPTER ONE

Understanding your mortgage

This chapter explains the different kinds of mortgages available, how they work and from whom you may be able to get your loan. It goes on to cover ways in which the government helps you pay your mortgage. If you are facing high mortgage payments and want to cut the cost, you must first sort out:

- how many mortgages you have (you could well have more than one);
- what kind of mortgages they are (that is, what arrangements you have made for repaying each one);
- what help you are receiving from the government.

This chapter will be particularly useful if you have not had much to do with your mortgage(s) until now; for instance, if you have been left on your own in the home by your partner. However, if you do understand your mortgage(s), you could move on to Chapter two, Chapter three and Chapter four to see how to increase your income, or to the rest of the book to see how to cut your costs, and simply refer back when necessary.

HOW MORTGAGES WORK

In this section a number of legal and technical terms which are essential to understand in using this book are explained. These words are highlighted in bold in the text to help you refer back to the explanations if you need to.

A **mortgage** is a type of loan which gives lenders the right to recover their money by taking over your home and selling it if you fail to make the agreed repayments.

Your payments are the instalments you pay to your lender every month. There will normally be two parts to each payment:

- **Interest** – this is the price you have to pay for borrowing the money. It is expressed as a percentage of the sum owing to the lender;

and *either*

- **capital** – this is the term used for the money you have borrowed and are paying back directly to your lender; *or*

- an **endowment premium** – this is a monthly payment which you make to a life assurance company. Instead of paying directly to your lender, you save with the life assurance company. The life assurance company agrees to pay back the full amount you have borrowed to your lender at the end of an agreed period (or on your death if you die before the end of that period).

A **mortgagee** is a person or institution (such as a building society or bank) who lends money secured against a property under a mortgage. Normally referred to as a 'lender'.

A **mortgagor** is a person who borrows money, either for house purchase or some other purpose, secured by a charge against property. Normally referred to as a 'borrower'.

The **term** is the word used for the number of years over which you have borrowed money and have agreed to pay it back.

The rights that a mortgage lender has against the borrower are secured by registering a **charge**, either at the appropriate District Land Registry or, if the land is unregistered, at the Land Charges Registry in Plymouth. In Scotland, charges are registered in the Land Register in Edinburgh. The existence of a charge has two important consequences:

- the lenders can apply to a court for an order to sell your home to get their money back if you do not make the agreed payments (or you break the terms of the mortgage agreement in some other way); *and*

- you must repay your lenders the sum outstanding on your mortgage when you sell your home. (Before a property can change hands the charges must be removed; when the charge is a mortgage, it will only be removed when the loan is repaid.) Every mortgage you have will be registered as a charge. These will be listed, usually in the order in which you borrowed the money, so that the first lender will have the **first charge**, the second lender will have the **second charge**, and so on. This is the order in which the lenders will be repaid if your home is sold.

The **equity** is the difference between the sale value of your home, and the value of the mortgage 'charged' against it. For example, if you sell your home for £75,000 and you had two loans, of which £35,000 is still owing to the building society who lent you the money to buy it in the first place, and £10,000 is still owing to the finance company who lent you the money to put in central heating and buy a car; the building society has the 'first charge' and takes the first £35,000, and the finance company has the 'second charge' and takes the next £10,000. The remainder is your 'equity', £30,000.

Negative equity is what you have if, after your house has been sold, you still owe more money to your lender, either because the value of the house has gone down since you originally borrowed money, or because you have accumulated arrears on the loan.

A **possession order** is an order by a court entitling a lender to take possession of a property and sell it to get their money back because the borrower has not kept up with her/his payments or is in breach of the mortgage agreement in some other way. The court may either grant an **outright** possession order, entitling the lender to take immediate possession, or a **suspended** possession order which will not be implemented as long as the borrower maintains payments at a particular level. A suspended possession order is not available in Scotland.

TYPES OF MORTGAGES

When you borrow money, methods of repayment vary with the type of mortgage. These are described below.

Capital repayment (or annuity) mortgages

If you have a capital repayment mortgage, your monthly payments are made up, in part, of the interest you pay on the amount borrowed and, in part, repayment of the loan itself (called capital). Unless the interest rate changes, your monthly payments remain the same throughout the period of your mortgage.

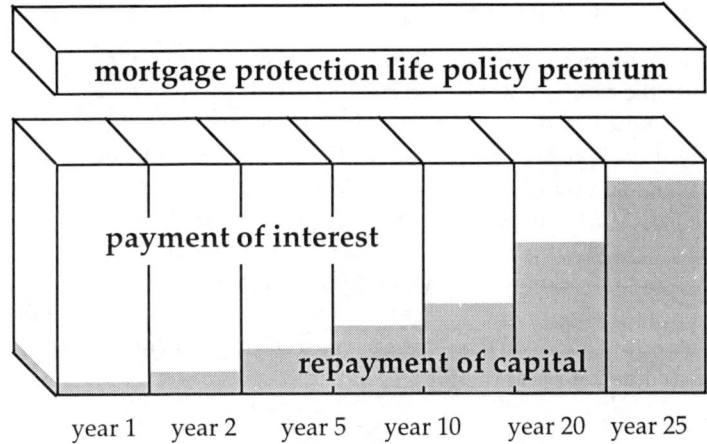

In the first year of your mortgage, most of your monthly payment is interest on the loan and only a tiny amount is paying off the capital. Your monthly mortgage payments in the second year will be the same, but the proportions of interest and capital will begin to change so that your payments will consist of slightly less interest than in the first year and slightly more capital. As each year goes by, you will pay off more of the amount borrowed. As you pay interest on a smaller and smaller amount, more capital is paid off and, by the end of the loan period, your payment is almost all capital with only a tiny amount of interest.

Some capital repayment mortgages require only a very small amount of the capital to be repaid in the first few years. The payment of capital is loaded into the remainder of the term so as to make the monthly payments less costly at the outset. These are called low-start capital repayment mortgages.

The top part of the diagram on page 3 shows a very important third part of your monthly payments. This is the small payment that makes sure that your family are not left with the worry of repaying the loan if you die before the end of the term. The payment is for a **mortgage protection policy** (see page 9). Your lender will offer to arrange mortgage protection cover when you take out a capital repayment mortgage, or you may arrange your own cover.

If you have dependants or other people for whom you wish to make provision after your death, it is a good idea to take out this sort of policy. But make sure that it *will* repay the loan, and that you are not excluded by the terms of the policy. You may be excluded if you have health problems, or are in a group regarded by insurance companies as having a high risk of HIV infection (these can be very widely drawn, and some companies include most single men, all people who have had an HIV test and people who have lived in Africa).

Endowment mortgages

Endowment mortgages are different from capital repayment mortgages because the capital is not repaid gradually year by year but is paid back all at once at the end of the mortgage term. To make sure that you will be able to pay it back at the end, you take out an **endowment policy** with a life assurance company. In return for your monthly payment of insurance premiums, the life assurance company agrees to pay the lender a lump sum at the end of your loan (or on your death if this is earlier).

You pay interest on the loan, and your insurance premium each month but, because you do not repay any of the money until the end of the term, the interest will remain the same each year. Your payments will only change if the interest rate rises or falls.

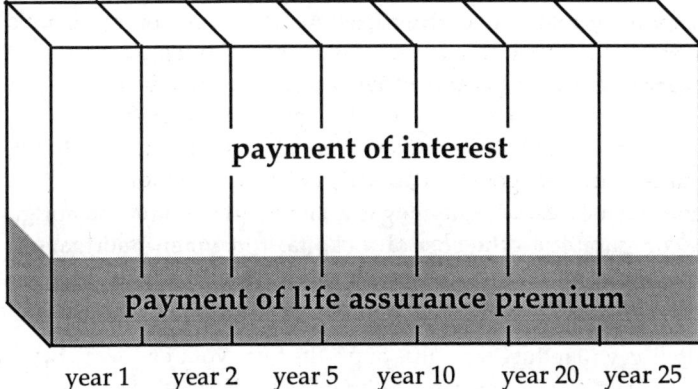

There are three different kinds of endowment life policy which can be used to repay a mortgage. Look at your own policy to find out which you have. The three kinds of endowment policy are:

- ☐ a **'guaranteed' or 'non-profit' endowment**: this is where the life assurance company agrees to pay the amount of money you borrowed at the end of the term (or on your death, if you die before then) and does no more than that. This policy probably offers the worst value for money. Many second mortgages are covered by this kind of endowment policy;

- ☐ a **'with profits' endowment**: this is where the life assurance company agrees to do two things. First, it will repay, at the end of the term, the money you borrowed. Second, it will give you some extra money which it calls 'profits', 'bonuses' or 'dividends'. You will have to pay higher premiums to get this extra sum. The company decides every few years what the bonuses should be and they are stored up for you. If you should die before the end of the mortgage term, the whole loan will be repaid.

   This kind of policy offers a built-in savings scheme but has the highest monthly premiums. A report in the Consumers' Association magazine *Which?* concluded that if you want to save, you would do better to invest in a separate savings scheme rather than link it to your mortgage;

- ☐ a **'low-cost' or 'build-up' endowment**: this is where you take out a 'with profits' policy for less than the amount you borrowed. The idea is that your bonuses will build up so that, by the end of the term, you will have enough to repay the loan and a bit extra for yourself. There is also an agreement that the whole loan will be repaid if you should die before the end of the term. Your monthly payments are lower than those of a full 'with profits' endowment but so are your savings. The premiums for a low-cost endowment are less than those for a guaranteed or non-profit policy.

Repayment or endowment mortgage?

Normally, capital repayment mortgages (see page 3) are best for most people because:

- [ ] although the monthly outgoings on a low-cost endowment mortgage can be comparable to the cost of a capital repayment mortgage, capital repayment mortgages are much more flexible if you have financial difficulties and need to rearrange your finances;
- [ ] inflation will reduce the value of profits from your endowment policy. In April 1988, *Which?* magazine estimated that, if inflation runs at 4 per cent, after 25 years, a £10,000 lump sum would be worth under £4,000 in terms of buying power.

Pension-linked mortgages

If you have a pension-linked mortgage it will work in a similar way to an endowment mortgage. You will make two monthly payments. One will consist of interest on the loan and the other a separate monthly insurance premium which will repay your loan at the end of the term, and, in addition, provide a pension on your retirement. On retirement you can convert part of your pension to a tax free lump sum which is used to pay off your mortgage. Pension mortgages are more expensive than endowment mortgages because, as well as repaying your loan, they also provide you with a pension. You should also remember that if you use part of your pension to pay off your mortgage, then you will obviously have a reduced pension.

Interest-only mortgages

If you have an interest-only mortgage then you will only be paying interest on your loan. This type of loan is designed for those approaching or over retirement age who cannot take out a long mortgage term. The amount borrowed is repaid on the sale of the property or on the death of the borrower. Most lenders will allow another interest-only loan if you move home, and may offer loan facilities to your relatives or inheritors if you should die and they wish to keep the property.

'Low-start' mortgages

These are designed to help borrowers over the early years of the term. The lender agrees to charge below the commercial interest rate for up to the first five years and then charges the standard interest rate at the end of this period. The lender will normally require the interest which has been unpaid in this initial period to be paid off over the remainder of the term.

These loans can be useful if you are sure that your income is going to increase sufficiently, by the time the full interest rate is charged, to meet the increased monthly payments. If your income does not increase sufficiently, you may find yourself overcommitted

Fixed interest rate mortgages

This type of loan is for those who feel able to gamble on changes in interest rates. In these loans the interest rate is fixed at the start of the loan, either for a number of years or for the whole term. If interest rates increase, then you end up paying less than the going rate. However, if interest rates drop then you are stuck paying over the odds. Lenders usually impose a charge of three months' or more interest if a borrower switches out of a fixed interest rate mortgage in the first five years.

Shared ownership mortgages

These are mortgages which allow you to purchase a share in a property. The share usually starts at 50 per cent, but can be lower. You take out a mortgage to enable you to buy your initial share and you will pay a 'market rent', set by the rent officer, on the share of the property you have not purchased. For example, if you initially purchase a 50 per cent share, in addition to your mortgage payments, you will pay 50 per cent of a market rent on the remaining share. Rent levels are set by the local rent officer.

Shared ownership schemes are offered by housing associations or sometimes local authorities. But the mortgage itself will usually come from a building society. If you take out a shared ownership mortgage, you will buy a 99-year lease which allows you to purchase additional shares (normally of 12.5 per cent or 25 per cent) as and when you can afford the additional mortgage payments. When you buy additional shares this is called 'staircasing'. The aim is that eventually the borrower will acquire 100 per cent of the property. From the outset the borrower is responsible for repairs, although this is reflected in a reduced rent on the share of the property still being rented.

Secured loans

You may have one or more secured loans in addition to your first mortgage. These loans are called secured loans because the lender will have registered

a charge (see page 2) on your home for the amount of the loan. In this way, the lender has secured the certainty of recovering the money lent, with interest, if you default on the payments. Secured loans may be taken out for any purpose and are normally repaid on a capital repayment basis, but interest rates will usually be higher than for your first mortgage. You are likely to have a shorter mortgage term on your secured loan and this, together with a higher interest rate, will make your monthly payments comparatively high. You should remember that although this type of loan can be taken out for a comparatively small sum of money, lenders under secured loans have the same rights to repossess your home as lenders on first mortgages. Most secured loans are regulated by the Consumer Credit Act 1974 (see page 83).

Business loans

If you have a loan to finance a business secured on your home, not only is this *not* going to be covered by the Consumer Credit Act, but it is also likely to be at a high rate of interest. If you have any problems with a business loan you should seek expert advice urgently (see Appendix 7).

Bridging loans

Unlike the types of mortgages described above, there is no arrangement for repaying a bridging loan built into your loan agreement. A bridging loan is only granted to 'bridge' the gap until money comes through from another source (this might be cash from the sale of another home, or it might be the advance of your mortgage money). You have to repay the loan as soon as the money is available, and you have to pay interest on the loan until then. The interest you have to pay will be higher than building society interest rates. Never take out a bridging loan unless you are absolutely certain that the amount of money you need will be forthcoming at a particular date. A bridging loan will not usually be granted for more than a year. When the agreed time is up you may be put under pressure to sell your home in order to repay (but see Chapter six).

TYPES OF INSURANCE POLICIES

You may have a number of different types of insurance policies linked to your mortgage. These include:

- **Endowment policies** (see page 4). Lenders selling endowment policies receive large commission payments from the insurance companies. There is strong evidence that this leads lenders and brokers to recommend endowment policies to borrowers for whom repayment mortgages would be more suitable. A report by the Consumers' Association in *Which?* magazine in May 1993 found that 'of 72 mortgage advisers who recommended a mortgage, 56 said an endowment was ... best ... In fact a repayment mortgage was at least as suitable as an endowment one.'

From January 1995 you will be told the full amount of commission and other costs deducted from your premiums when you buy a policy. You will also be told the effect of these payments on the value of your investment if you surrender it before it matures.

In the last two years, a number of insurance companies have warned borrowers that, because of the low return on investments, their current low-cost endowment policies cannot be guaranteed to repay all the money that they borrowed.

Because of these factors, a number of lenders have decided in the last year to cease selling endowment mortgages, but they still remain the commonest form of mortgage.

- **Mortgage protection policies** (see page 4). These can be good value for money if you are sure that your mortgage loan *will* be covered in the event of your death.

- **Payment protection plans**. These are meant to meet your mortgage payments in the event of your becoming ill or losing your job. There have, however, been many cases of these policies being sold to people who are not covered by the small print, which might exclude self-employed people or those accepting voluntary redundancy (even if the only alternative is compulsory redundancy on less favourable terms!).

    The growth in claims under these policies during the recession has also led insurers to increase the premiums steeply. Typically, you will now pay between £10 and £20 for each £100 of payment covered. If you have, or are considering, taking out one of these policies, read the small print to check that you are fully covered, and remember that your lender will receive substantial commission for selling this policy to you.

- **Mortgage indemnity insurance**. Your lender will insist on this being taken out if you borrow more than 70 to 80 per cent of the value of your property. This policy is not for your benefit but for the benefit of your lender and will allow them to reclaim a proportion of their losses from the insurer should you default on your mortgage. This will not mean that your debt is cleared, though, and the insurer will be able to pursue you for the money they have paid to your lender (see Chapter 9 for more detail).

- **Building and contents insurance.** Your lender will insist on your property being insured against fire and other damage. If you do not arrange your insurance through your lender, they will charge you a fee, normally of around £25. Consumer organisations argue that this is a restrictive practice and if you can find cheaper insurance elsewhere but cannot afford this fee, you should ask your lender to waive it. Many lenders will also arrange contents insurance, but if you can arrange this for less elsewhere, there is nothing to stop you from doing so.

In England and Wales, if you are buying a leasehold property, the freeholder is responsible for arranging building insurance. Your solicitor should check during the conveyancing that adequate insurance cover is in place. You have the right to request details of building insurance from your freeholder under the Landlord and Tenant Act 1987.

TYPES OF LENDERS

Lenders of money guaranteed by a mortgage are called mortgagees, and borrowers are called mortgagors. To avoid confusion, this guide talks about 'lenders' and 'borrowers'.

There are several kinds of lenders. They can vary greatly as to the kind of mortgage they will offer, the rates of interest they will charge, and the maximum number of years over which the loan can be paid back.

Building societies

Building societies lend in two ways:

- first mortgages for buying a home;
- second mortgages for improving a home, buying a car or for some other purpose. Second mortgages are likely to be at a higher interest rate and over a shorter term.

Building society mortgages are among the cheapest available and they allow long repayment terms (sometimes up to 35 years). All major building societies belong to the Building Societies' Association and are members of the Council of Mortgage Lenders (see Appendix 7 for addresses). However, individual societies are free to set their own interest rates. Societies may have different lending policies and often local branch managers have some discretion in deciding what to do in individual cases.

Local authorities

Local authorities have the power to lend money to enable people to buy, improve or repair their homes. Normally they will only lend if they can register the **first charge** (see page 2), but they do have the power to take the **second charge** on loans for improvements or repairs. They generally lend money on older properties and may charge higher rates of interest than building societies. They only lend on a capital repayment basis. Local authorities should be particularly helpful if one of their borrowers has difficulty in making payments, as they may have to rehouse someone evicted for non-payment (see page 138).

However, because of financial cutbacks in recent years, most local authorities are reluctant to use their powers to lend money on mortgages. A number of authorities have even sold their 'portfolios' of mortgages to building societies or banks for cash. This means that borrowers suddenly find themselves borrowing money from another body with different lending policies.

If council tenants exercise the 'right to buy' their council home, a local authority is obliged to provide a mortgage. Normally, however, this is done by arranging a building society mortgage.

Insurance companies

Granting mortgages is not the main business of insurance companies. Many of them will not grant first mortgages at all, or will consider them only for more expensive properties. They lend on endowment and pension mortgages. The most common way in which insurance companies are involved in the granting of mortgages is by providing endowment life assurance policies to people borrowing on that basis from building societies. In addition, insurance companies sometimes lend 'topping-up' mortgages and take a second charge where a building society has the first charge. This usually happens when the building society has refused to lend as much as the borrower needs. Only take out a second mortgage if you are absolutely sure that the first lender will not lend you more. It is important to work out how much the second mortgage will cost and whether you can afford the extra payments. If you must have a second mortgage, you will usually get a much cheaper one from an insurance company than from a finance company.

Banks

Banks lend in two ways:

- ☐ first mortgages for buying or improving a home are normally over a 20- or 25-year period at interest rates similar to those of the building societies;

- second loans for any purpose – for example, for installing central heating or buying a car – are likely to be over a shorter period, such as 10 years. These loans will be secured on your home. They are relatively expensive because the monthly payments need to be high to repay the loan in such a short time, and are likely to be at a higher interest rate than a first loan.

Finance companies

You may have bought your home with a finance company mortgage, or you may have borrowed from them later with a second mortgage to pay for central heating, a car, or furniture for example. Your payments are probably very high because some finance companies charge interest rates of up to 50 per cent (you may have to look carefully at the small print to find the true rate), and because they will only lend over a fairly short term, at most about 15 years. Smaller finance companies and credit brokers have been known to charge as much as 68 per cent rate of interest. You may also find that you were charged a fee for the mortgage when you took it out (which could be 10 per cent of your loan), and that you are also paying interest on this fee.

A finance company mortgage could land you in serious trouble, both because the monthly costs are often higher than you think at the beginning, and also because, once you start missing payments, arrears build up very quickly. If you try to pay back (or 'redeem') the whole loan, you may find that you owe far more than you originally borrowed. Generally, where the sum borrowed is less than £15,000, the loan will be covered by the Consumer Credit Act 1974. This Act gives the local county court powers to regulate the rate of repayment and to change the terms of the loan agreement (see Chapter six).

GOVERNMENT HELP WITH YOUR MORTGAGE

The government provides assistance for those paying off a mortgage if the money is used to buy the home. The help takes the form of giving tax relief on the interest payments that are made and is available for the first £30,000 of the loan. Under the MIRAS (Mortgage Interest Relief At Source) system, introduced in April 1983, most borrowers with loans of up to £30,000 pay mortgage interest to their lender at a reduced rate.

Until April 1994 this was equivalent to the basic rate of income tax (25 per cent). In April 1994 this relief was cut to 20 per cent of the interest rate and from April 1995 it will be reduced again to 15 per cent. Tax relief is deducted by the lender on interest up to £30,000. Interest payments net of tax relief are made direct to the lender. See Appendix 1 to find out how to calculate the effect of MIRAS on your payments.

From 1 August 1988, tax relief was limited to £30,000 per property. However, unmarried mortgage sharers whose loan contracts were entered into before 1 August 1988 will continue to receive tax relief on up to £30,000 each. They will lose this 'double tax relief' if they get married or if they take out a new mortgage – for example, to buy a new home or to extend their existing mortgage. For general information on the MIRAS system, see leaflet IR63 available from your tax office.

CHAPTER TWO

How to increase your income: working full time

If you are encountering financial difficulties, you should see if there are ways of increasing your weekly income so that you can pay your mortgage costs and keep your home. You should also try to cut your housing costs (see Chapter five). There is a wide range of social security benefits, some of which you may be entitled to claim. This book concentrates on the main means-tested benefits (ie, those which depend on your income and capital). For further details of all social security benefits see CPAG's *National Welfare Benefits Handbook* and *Rights Guide to Non-Means-Tested Benefits* (see Appendix 9). This chapter explains the benefits you should claim for yourself and/or your family if you or your partner are working full-time (16 hours or more each week). The rules are broadly the same whether you are working for an employer or are self-employed. If you are already claiming some or all of these benefits, use this chapter to check that you are getting the right amount. The figures given are correct for the period between April 1994 and April 1995. You may feel that you are not quite sure whether you qualify for some of the benefits. The best advice is, if in doubt, claim. You lose nothing by applying, and the extra money you gain may make the difference between being able to stay in your home and having to sell because you cannot pay the mortgage. Most, but not all, of the benefits described in this chapter can be claimed from the Benefits Agency.

Note: There are special rules for people who have come to this country from abroad (whether within the European Union or outside it). If this applies to you, it is very important that you get advice from one of the organisations listed in Appendix 7 *before* you claim any social security benefit.

FAMILY CREDIT

Family credit (FC) is a weekly cash payment intended to help families on low wages. It can amount to a substantial sum each week, and you may be surprised at how much income you can have and still get some FC. For example, a family with two teenage children at school might have an income of around £190 per week net and still get some FC. (See Appendix 2 to help

you work out whether you could qualify.)
You can claim FC if:

- [ ] you have one or more dependent children under 16 normally living with you (or under 19 if they are in 'relevant' education – that is, up to 'A' level or its equivalent); *and*

- [ ] you or your partner (if you have one) normally work(s) at least 16 hours a week. This includes any paid meal breaks, and can be made up from more than one part-time job; *and*

- [ ] you and your partner together have no more than £8,000 in savings or other capital.

In assessing how much capital you have, the Benefits Agency will take into account money in a bank or building society, savings certificates, shares and property, among other things. However, some capital will be ignored, including the surrender value of life assurance (including endowment) policies, and the value of the home you live in. (For more details about the capital rules, see Appendix 4.)

How and when to claim

Get the Family Credit Claim Pack (FC1) from a citizens advice bureau, job centre, post office or local Benefits Agency office. It includes the claim form and a return envelope. Don't be put off by the claim form. It may look quite long but you will probably find the questions easy to answer. We give some hints on filling in the form on page 16. Usually, in a heterosexual couple, it is the woman who has to claim.

If there are no complications, you will receive an order book within a few weeks of sending off your forms. It will normally last for 26 weeks, starting from the Tuesday after the Benefits Agency receives the form. You then cash an order form from the book each week at the post office. You can ask for FC to be paid directly into your bank or building society account. You can also ask for an 'interim payment' while your claim is being processed.

Timing your claim

If you are already receiving FC at the time of the annual April increases, you will not receive the increase until your current award runs out after 26 weeks and you re-apply. For example, if the FC award began in December 1992, you would not benefit from the new rates until your current award runs out in June 1993 and you claim again.

If you are thinking of claiming FC, it may be worth delaying your claim until April because you may be better off overall by foregoing benefit for a few weeks, then qualifying for six months at the higher rate. It may also be worth considering delaying your claim if your circumstances are about to change in a way that might lead to a higher amount of FC – for example, if you are about to take a drop in income, or have another child or one of your children is about to reach their eleventh, sixteenth or eighteenth birthday.

You may want to discuss the merits of delaying a claim with an advice agency (see Appendix 7 for addresses).

Claim family credit however small your entitlement

It is always worth claiming FC, even if the weekly amount is the lowest possible – that is, 50 pence. This is because you will only need to show your FC book to receive other benefits free for all the family (see page 25). You may also get legal help, free or at a reduced cost, under the Legal Aid Scheme (see Appendix 6) and reduced price powdered milk if you have a child under one year old. FC will also mean you qualify for help with maternity and funeral costs from the social fund (see page 49) and for other needs (see page 50).

Filling in the application form

Check below to make sure that you remember to include everything when you fill in the form:

- ☐ Your earnings will have to be checked. So, if you are an employee, you are asked to send your last six weekly wage slips or last three monthly salary slips. If your partner works, send his as well (or instead, if you do not work). FC can only be backdated if you have a good reason for not claiming earlier, so *do not delay* claiming because you do not have your wage slips. Write on the form that you will send them later. If you do have details, you will probably need them for claiming other benefits, so try and get photocopies made and send those instead of the originals. If you have only just started a job, the Benefits Agency will ask your employer to estimate what your earnings are likely to be over the next five weeks. If you, or your partner, are self-employed, you will be asked to provide information about the business and accounts (or a statement of earnings and expenses).

- ☐ It is possible that your most recent wages may have been higher than usual, perhaps because of extra overtime or seasonal work. There are special rules which cater for this sort of situation – broadly, earnings 20 per cent above (or below) the recent average are ignored. Explain the position on the form.

☐ Similarly, you or your partner may have been paid more in the recent past than you are earning now and expect to earn in the near future. This could be because you have just cut down your hours of work, or you have changed your job and are getting a lower wage. If so, write on the form that you want FC to be assessed on the basis of your earnings as at the date of your claim because these now represent your normal earnings. Offer to send the Benefits Agency your wage slips for the next six weeks when you get them. Seek advice if the Benefits Agency refuses to award you FC (see Appendix 7 for the addresses of advice agencies).

☐ If you, or your partner's, hours of work fluctuate, the Benefits Agency will take an average, to check that they add up to at least 16 hours a week. If there is a regular cycle (eg, a monthly shift rota), then an average will be taken over the period of that cycle. If there is no pattern, the Benefits Agency will use the last five weeks, or any other appropriate period.

☐ You may be due to receive maintenance payments which arrive irregularly, or not at all. If this happens, the Benefits Agency should take an average of the payments you have received in the last 13 weeks before your claim, and treat that as your normal income. However, with child support maintenance payments, if the average figure is more than the amount assessed by the Child Support Agency, you take the assessment figure instead. (See Chapter eight for more about child support.) If any maintenance payments have been irregular, explain on the claim form and give details of the payments received over the past 13 weeks. Fifteen pounds of your maintenance payments is ignored as income.

☐ Capital below £3,000 does not affect FC. Any capital between £3,000 and £8,000 is treated as giving you an assumed income of £1 per week for each £250 (or part of £250). For example, savings of £3,450 would be treated as giving you an income of £2 per week. This is known as **tariff income**.

☐ If you think you should have been receiving FC before now, your claim can be backdated for up to a year, *provided you had 'good cause' for not claiming before* – for example, you have been ill, or you were given wrong information by the Benefits Agency. Ignorance of your right to make a claim is not generally considered to be 'good cause'. However, if you had good reason to believe that you were not entitled, this may be 'good cause' (see Appendix 7 for the addresses of advice agencies). Anyway, there is no harm in asking to backdate your claim, whatever the likely outcome.

☐ You include in your claim children who normally live with you. Children who spend a short time away from home – for instance, because they are in hospital or staying with relatives – may still be regarded as normally living with you.

How much will you receive?

This depends on how much your weekly income exceeds the 'threshold', which is fixed by parliament each year. The threshold is £71.70 until April 1995. If your income does not exceed the threshold, then you receive an amount known as 'maximum family credit'. This amount varies according to the number and ages of your children. As your income rises above the threshold, your maximum FC is reduced by 70 pence in the pound. So, if your net income is £10 over the threshold, your maximum FC would be reduced by £7 (see Appendix 2 for details of the calculation).

How to calculate your weekly income

First, take your full weekly earnings before any deductions, then subtract the tax, national insurance, and half of any pension scheme contributions you pay. If the earnings are from self-employment, you can also deduct reasonable expenses. This figure is used as your **net earnings**. If you are a married or unmarried couple, both incomes will be counted.

Second, add to this figure any maintenance payments (disregarding £15 a week) and national insurance benefits you receive, but do not include any of the following:

- ☐ child benefit;
- ☐ one parent benefit;
- ☐ housing benefit;
- ☐ attendance allowance;
- ☐ disability living allowance;
- ☐ disability working allowance;
- ☐ council tax benefit;
- ☐ income support;
- ☐ social fund payments;
- ☐ educational maintenance allowances;
- ☐ money paid to you by someone who lives with you on a non-commercial basis ('non-dependants', see page 41);

- [ ] maternity allowance or statutory maternity pay;
- [ ] guardian's allowance.

If you are self-employed, your net profit over the previous year or so is usually used to work out your income, although a more recent period can be used if that would be a better reflection of your normal earnings.

For an example of how to calculate family credit, see Appendix 2.

The government has announced that, from 4 October 1994, childcare costs can sometimes be deducted from earnings. This also applies to disability working allowance (see below), housing benefit (see page 24) and council tax benefit (see Chapter four). Costs of up to £40 per week can be offset against earnings, whether you or your partner are employed or self-employed. The rule will apply if you are a lone parent or both you and your partner work (or one of you works and the other is too ill or disabled to work). It is only childcare for children under 11 which counts. The childcare must be provided by a registered childminder, day nursery or similar body. If the child is aged between eight and ten, the childcare can also be provided by a school or local authority (out of school hours). Forty pounds is the maximum deduction that can be made, no matter how many children you have receiving childcare. With family credit, the new rules could mean up to an extra £28 benefit a week.

Challenging the decision

You can appeal within three months of the date of the decision (or later if there are 'special reasons' why a late appeal should be heard – see page 47). You will then be able to put your case to a Social Security Appeal Tribunal, but you should get advice about this before you go (see Appendix 7 for the addresses of advice agencies).

DISABILITY WORKING ALLOWANCE

Disability working allowance (DWA) is a benefit for low-paid workers who have a disability. It tops up your wages if you are in full-time work (at least 16 hours a week). DWA was introduced in April 1992. The Benefits Agency publicity did not explain that some claimants may be worse off if they receive DWA. Nor did it mention the potential disadvantages of receiving DWA. In particular, some disabled workers can claim income support even if they work 16 hours or more a week. As you receive housing costs as part of your income support (see pages 31-33), but not as part of your DWA, you may be better off taking this option.

Check to see if you satisfy the basic rules for claiming and then seek advice about the advantages and disadvantages of doing so (see Appendix 7 for the addresses of advice agencies).

Who can claim

You can claim DWA if:

- [ ] your savings and capital are no more than £16,000 (for how savings and capital are calculated, see Appendix 4); *and*
- [ ] you work for at least 16 hours a week; *and*
- [ ] you have a disability which puts you at a disadvantage in getting a job (see below); *and*
- [ ] you are, or have recently been, getting a sickness or disability benefit (see below), or you have an invalid 'trike' or similar vehicle; *and*
- [ ] you are not getting family credit; *and*
- [ ] you are 16 or older; *and*
- [ ] your income is low enough. (Income is calculated in a similar way to family credit, see Appendix 2.)

How to claim

You claim in writing using the DWA claim pack, available from the Benefits Agency, Job Centre, post office or citizens advice bureau.

The disability and disadvantage test

To qualify for DWA, you must have a disability which puts you at a disadvantage in getting a job. Both physical and mental disability count. If you are claiming for the first time, or after a period of two years when you were not getting DWA, you simply have to sign a declaration that this applies to you. This will be accepted *unless* the information given on your claim form is contradictory, *or* the adjudication officer has other evidence about you which indicates that you do not fulfil that condition. For all other claims, you fulfil this condition if one of the following applies:

- [ ] you are paid one of the following benefits (or its Northern Ireland equivalent):
    - the highest or middle-rate care component or the higher-rate mobility component of the disability living allowance;

HOW TO INCREASE YOUR INCOME: WORKING FULL TIME

- attendance allowance;
- industrial disablement benefit or a war pension, where you are at least 80 per cent disabled;
- mobility supplement;

- [ ] you have an invalid 'trike' or similar vehicle;

- [ ] you were paid severe disablement allowance (or the Northern Ireland equivalent) for at least one day in the eight weeks prior to your 'initial claim'. **Initial claim** means your first successful claim for DWA, or a new claim where you have not been getting DWA during the last two years;

- [ ] you cannot keep your balance without holding on to something when standing;

- [ ] you cannot walk 100 metres on level ground without stopping or suffering severe pain. You are expected to use walking aids such as crutches, a stick, a frame or an artificial limb if you normally use these;

- [ ] you cannot use your hands behind your back (as you would when putting on a jacket or tucking your shirt in);

- [ ] you cannot extend your hands forwards in order to shake hands with someone without difficulty;

- [ ] you cannot put your hands up to your head without difficulty (as when putting on a hat);

- [ ] you cannot pick up a coin of $2\,^1/_2$ cm diameter because you lack normal dexterity in both hands;

- [ ] you cannot pick up a full one litre jug and pour into a cup from it without difficulty;

- [ ] you cannot turn either of your hands sideways through 180 degrees;

- [ ] you are registered blind or partially-sighted;

- [ ] you cannot read 16-point print from more than 20 cm distance, even when wearing your normal glasses, if any;

- [ ] you cannot hear a telephone ring when in the same room, even with your hearing aid, if any;

- [ ] you cannot hear someone talking in a loud voice when the room is quiet and they are only two metres away from you;

- [ ] people who know you well have difficulty understanding what you say;

- ☐ you have difficulty understanding a person you know well;
- ☐ at least once a year you lose consciousness during a fit, or go into a coma;
- ☐ you have a mental illness for which you are getting regular treatment;
- ☐ you are often confused or forgetful due to mental disability;
- ☐ you cannot do simple addition and subtraction;
- ☐ you hit people, or damage property or cannot socialise because of your mental disability;
- ☐ you cannot manage an eight-hour working day or a five-day week because of your medical condition or because you suffer from severe pain;
- ☐ following illness or accident you are undergoing rehabilitation. You can only use this condition to qualify on an initial claim (see page 21).

If you fulfil the disability test for DWA because you were paid one of the specified benefits (see pages 20-21), or have an invalid trike, you will nevertheless be refused DWA if there is evidence that none of the other disability conditions are fulfilled.

Receipt of a sickness or disability benefit

To qualify for DWA you must also be, or have been, receiving a sickness or disability benefit. You are entitled to DWA if, *when you claim*, you are receiving:

- ☐ disability living allowance;
- ☐ attendance allowance, or an increase of your industrial disablement benefit or war pension for attendance needs;
- ☐ a corresponding benefit from Northern Ireland.

Alternatively, you qualify if, for at least one day in the eight weeks prior to your claim, you were getting:

- ☐ invalidity benefit or severe disablement allowance;
- ☐ income support, housing benefit or council tax benefit, but only if your applicable amount included the disability premium (or higher pensioner premium because of disability or incapacity). For an explanation of applicable amounts and more about premiums, see page 31 and Appendix 3;
- ☐ a corresponding benefit from Northern Ireland.

You can also meet this condition if you have an invalid trike or similar vehicle when you claim DWA.

Calculating disability working allowance

DWA is calculated by first working our your **maximum disability working allowance**. You then compare your **income**, calculated in a similar way to family credit (see Appendix 2) with your **applicable amount** which is a set figure of:

☐ £43.00 (single claimants); *or*

☐ £71.70 (couples or lone parents).

If your income is no more than your applicable amount you receive the maximum DWA. If it is more, you get the maximum DWA minus 70 per cent of the difference between your income and the applicable amount.

The **maximum DWA** is made up of allowances for each member of your family. These are as follows:

single claimant	£46.05
couple/lone parent	£63.75
child aged:	
under 11	£11.20
11-15	£18.55
16-17	£23.05
18	£32.20

Example
Winston is 19 and single. He works 25 hours per week. His income for DWA purposes is £65. He has no savings.
His maximum DWA is £46.05
His income exceeds the applicable amount of £43.00 by £22.00. Thus his maximum DWA is reduced by £15.40 (70% x £22.00) and he is paid £30.65 per week.
If his income had been below £43.00 he would have received the maximum DWA.

No allowance is given for a child who has:

☐ capital of over £3,000;

☐ a weekly income (excluding maintenance) which is greater than their allowance;

☐ been in hospital or local authority residential accommodation for the 52 weeks prior to your claim because of physical or mental illness or handicap.

HOUSING BENEFIT

Housing benefit is paid by local authorities to people who pay rent to occupy their homes. Most homeowners do not therefore qualify for housing benefit. 'Rent', for these purposes, does not cover the 'ground rent' payable under a long lease.

However, some home-owners are partly buying and partly renting their homes under a 'shared ownership' arrangement (see page 7). You can, therefore, claim housing benefit for the part you pay as 'rent' under a shared ownership scheme. Ask the local authority to send you a housing benefit claim form. The amount of help you get will depend on your income, savings and who lives in your household.

Note: you cannot get housing benefit for 'co-ownership' schemes. One of the advice agencies in Appendix 7 will be able to advise you whether your scheme is 'shared ownership' or 'co-ownership'.

For more information about housing benefit, see the SHAC/CIH *Guide to Housing Benefit and Council Tax Benefit* and CPAG's *National Welfare Benefits Handbook* (listed in Appendix 9).

COUNCIL TAX BENEFIT

If you are eligible for council tax benefit, you will either have to pay less council tax or none at all. See Chapter 4 for information about council tax benefit.

EDUCATION BENEFITS

School clothing

Some local authorities give grants for school uniforms and for other items of clothing and footwear that your children may need. Apply to the local education office (the school secretary or the town hall will give you the address). The amount you receive may vary considerably and so does the level of income below which you qualify, the number of grants you can have in any one year, and the way you receive them. You may find that you get a voucher that you have to exchange at one particular shop. If you cannot get all you need at that shop, you may then have to wait for another voucher to be made out for a different shop. This could mean weeks of delay, so do claim in good time before term begins. You could also contact your local authority councillors and try to encourage them to improve the local scheme or introduce one, if the local authority does not operate one at present.

Study grants for children over 16

If your child stays on at school, you may qualify for an **educational maintenance allowance** from your local authority. Again, the amount varies. There is a similar grant, called a minor award, for children who leave school but go full time to a technical college. Claim at the education office of your local authority.

School fares

If you have children under eight who travel more than two miles to school, or children over eight who travel more than three miles, you should claim free passes for them from your local authority. This is the general rule, but each authority also has the power to pay any other fare that seems reasonable. For example, you might get help if your child has to travel slightly less than the stated distances, or if the increased cost of fares creates a special difficulty for you.

HEALTH BENEFITS

Family credit gives you automatic entitlement to the following benefits for yourself and your family:

- ☐ free prescriptions;
- ☐ free dental treatment;
- ☐ 'full-value' vouchers for glasses or contact lenses;
- ☐ free wigs and fabric support;
- ☐ refunds of fares to hospital for treatment;
- ☐ reduced prices for powdered milk if you have a child under one year old.

Children under 16 qualify automatically for free prescriptions, as do children under 19 in full-time education. Dental care is free for all under 18-year-olds and for people in full-time education under 19. Children up to 16, or under 19 who are still in full-time education, can also get certain types of glasses free.

In addition, you and any teenage children may receive free or reduced cost health benefits on grounds of low income (in other words, even if you are not getting family credit). Ask at your local Benefits Agency office or post office for form AG1.

Points to note

- [ ] If in doubt, make a claim for help towards health service charges.

- [ ] If you do not qualify for help with prescriptions, you may save money by buying a prescription 'season ticket'. As at August 1994, this costs £24.60 for four months or £67.70 a year. If you need more than five items in the next four months, or more than fourteen in the next year, you will save money. Get form FP95 (EC95 in Scotland) from a post office, chemist or social security office.

SOCIAL FUND PAYMENTS

You may be entitled to a social fund crisis loan to help meet expenses in an emergency or disaster (see page 51). In addition, if you are getting family credit, disability working allowance, housing benefit or council tax benefit, you can apply for a social fund funeral grant; and if you get family credit or disability working allowance, you can also apply for a social fund maternity grant (see page 49).

OTHER BENEFITS AND GRANTS

If you are disabled, or care for a disabled person, there are a number of benefits to which you may be entitled even if you have not paid national insurance contributions. You can also get child benefit if you have a child under 16, or under 19 if s/he is in full-time secondary education, living with you, and in certain other circumstances too.

If you are getting family credit, disability working allowance, housing benefit or council tax benefit, you can apply for a Home Energy Efficiency Scheme grant (see page 90) or a grant for 'minor works assistance' (see page 87). You should get advice from one of the organisations listed in Appendix 7, and see CPAG's *Rights Guide to Non-Means-Tested Benefits* (see Appendix 9).

CHAPTER THREE

How to increase your income: not working full time

If neither you nor your partner are in work, or either or both of you only work part-time, this chapter will help you find ways of increasing your income. 'Part-time' means a job which you or your partner have for less than 16 hours a week. (If you or your partner work for 16 or more hours per week, see Chapter two for details about other benefits.) Sometimes you can work more than 16 hours and still get income support. This applies, for example, to some disabled people and some childminders. You should get advice about this (see Appendix 7). This chapter will help you discover the ways in which you can raise money to help meet your housing costs, but do check through Chapter five to make sure you have reduced those costs as far as possible.

Most of the help outlined in this chapter comes in the form of benefits paid by the Benefits Agency or your local authority. Amounts of benefit usually go up each year and where we give figures, these refer to the amounts set for April 1994 to April 1995. First look at the headings and the brief introduction to each type of benefit and make a note of the ones which might apply to you. Then go back to check for fuller details of the conditions attached to those benefits. You may not be sure whether you qualify for some of the benefits. The best advice is – if in doubt, claim. You lose nothing by applying and the extra money you gain may make the difference between being able to stay in your home and having to sell because you cannot pay the mortgage. However, if you have come to this country from abroad, the note on page 14 applies to you.

If not working or not working full-time is a new situation for you, you may have been told that, because your family circumstances have changed, you cannot afford to stay on in your home and that you should sell up and move out. It may be that you are sick, have been made redundant, have only part-time work or have been left by your partner. If you do want to keep your home, advice to sell and move can sometimes be disastrous and you should never do this without first looking at all the possible ways of staying where you are.

Faced with problems with your housing costs you and/or your partner will be particularly anxious to take up or return to full-time work in order to raise extra income. Before taking such a step, however, you should consider what effect this may have on any benefits you are receiving. Check with one of the agencies mentioned in Appendix 7 that you really will be better off working full-time.

INCOME SUPPORT

Most of this chapter is concerned with **income support**. This is the main benefit for people not working or where they and their partner each work less than 16 hours per week. It can be paid on its own or to 'top up' other income you have, such as sickness benefit or unemployment benefit, although most benefits will be taken into account in assessing your total weekly income. In most cases, you will be able to get payment of some or all of the interest portion of your mortgage. Don't worry if you think your outgoings are too high; most people can cut these costs in one of the ways described in Chapter five.

If your income is too high you will not qualify for income support, so see page 51 for other benefits to claim.

Who can claim

Any person aged 18 or over (and some 16- and 17-year-olds) whose weekly income is below a certain level may claim income support. There are a number of exceptions to this general rule. The main ones are that you cannot claim if:

- ☐ either you or your partner work 16 hours or more a week; *or*
- ☐ you and your partner have capital of more than £8,000.

> **Special note for separated partners:** If you leave the home you own or jointly own after the breakdown of your relationship, your share of the value of the house will be ignored for 26 weeks when calculating how much capital you have. If you make efforts to sell the home, or take legal action to allow you to move back in, then it can be ignored for longer (see Appendix 4 for more details).

To work out how much capital you have, the Benefits Agency will take into account things like money in a bank or building society, savings certificates, shares and property. However, some capital will be ignored, including the surrender value of life assurance (including endowment) policies, and the value of the home in which you live. For more details about the capital rules, see Appendix 4. If you own, or partly own, a home in which you no longer live – for example, because of a divorce or separation – you should get advice from one of the organisations listed in Appendix 7.

Many claimants of income support have to 'sign on' at the unemployment benefit office in order to receive benefit. There are, however, many groups of people who need not sign on, including lone parents with children under 16, those unable to work because they are ill or because they are looking after a severely disabled person, and people aged 60 or over.

Only one partner can claim on behalf of a couple. You can choose which of you makes the claim, but if one of you is too ill or disabled to work, then it is often best for that person to be the claimant as it may mean you get more income support. It is possible to swap the claimant role between partners.

All these rules apply to both married and unmarried couples living together. A man and woman will be treated as a couple by the Benefits Agency if it is thought they are 'living together as husband and wife'. This is sometimes known as the 'cohabitation rule'. The Benefits Agency may say that you are cohabiting when you do not agree that you are. You should appeal if this means that your income support is withdrawn or your claim refused. For advice on this, you could contact one of the organisations listed in Appendix 7.

How and when to claim

You should claim immediately if you think that you might be entitled to income support, since you cannot normally get payment for a period before you claim.

Income support can, however, be backdated if you can show 'good cause' for your claim being late. This means that you have a good reason why you did not claim. If your belief that you were not entitled is a reasonable one given the circumstances, that can be 'good cause'. You may wish to seek advice about this (see Appendix 7 for the addresses of advice agencies).

How you claim depends on whether or not you have to sign on.

If you have to sign on you should claim income support by going to the local Employment Service Office (Unemployment Benefit Office) and asking for form B1. This is a detailed questionnaire which you should fill in and send to the address you will be given. Form B1 also includes a separate form to claim council tax benefit from the local authority. You will be asked to produce various documents which confirm the information you give on form B1 – for example, bank statements, savings books, child benefit order books and details of any other income you have. If you have a mortgage, you will be asked to fill in form MI12 and to give this to your lender, who adds in information about your mortgage and returns the form to the Benefits Agency.

If you do *not* have to sign on you should contact your local Benefits Agency. You can telephone them and ask to claim, but it is safer to write and keep a dated copy of your letter. You need not write in detail as the Benefits Agency will send you a full questionnaire. If you need money urgently, it is probably best to visit the office immediately. The form asks you to state all your personal details so that the Benefits Agency can work out if you are entitled and, if so, to how much. Be sure to tell them everything. Again, if you have a mortgage, you have to fill in form MI12. If you have reading or writing problems, or some other reason why you would rather explain your circumstances to a Benefits Agency officer than fill in a form, let the Benefits Agency know and they should arrange for you to come to their offices for an interview, or send someone out to visit you. They may also arrange an interview if the information you put on the form needs clarification. It is a good idea to write out a statement of your situation to hand in at the interview if you have not already written a full account of your position in a letter or on the appropriate forms. If possible, keep a dated copy.

How payment is made

If you are entitled to income support, the date on which you will first be paid benefit depends on what other benefit(s) you may already be receiving. Most pensioners are paid weekly in advance – normally on a Monday. Most other people, except people signing on, are paid weekly in arrears. People who sign on as unemployed are usually paid fortnightly in arrears.

You will be sent a brief breakdown of how your benefit is calculated. You can ask for a more comprehensive explanation of your benefit assessment and use this to check your benefit against pages 31-33 in this guide.

At the same time as telling you about your income support entitlement, the Benefits Agency will, if appropriate, send the council tax benefit form to the local authority confirming that you are receiving income support. If you receive income support you will get what is called 'maximum council tax benefit' (see page 55). If you stop receiving income support you will have to make a fresh claim for council tax benefit direct to the local authority. See Chapter four for more information about council tax benefit.

How income support works

Because the income support scheme is so complicated, you should not just rely on the Benefits Agency to calculate your benefit correctly. You may not have received all the premiums to which you are entitled (see below), or they might have made a mistake about your income, so you should check the calculations carefully. If you are dissatisfied with the decision, you can appeal to a Social Security Appeal Tribunal (see page 47) within three months (or longer if there are 'special reasons' why a late appeal should be heard). See Appendix 7 for the addresses of agencies which can give you further advice.

How much will you receive?

The Benefits Agency will work out your applicable amount (what the law says you need to live on each week) and your income (the money you have coming in each week). If your income is less than the applicable amount, you will be awarded income support to make up the difference. If your income is more than your applicable amount, you will not get any income support (but see page 51 for details of other benefits you may be able to claim).

Your applicable amount

Your applicable amount is divided up into three parts (see Appendix 3 for the rates until April 1995):

- ☐ **Personal allowances** cover the day-to-day living expenses of you, your partner and any dependent children. A dependent child is one for whom you get child benefit, and is:
  - under 16; *or*
  - aged between 16 and 18, if still in full-time education (up to 'A' level or its equivalent); *or*
  - a 16/17-year-old who has finished education *but* for whom you can still claim child benefit. This is known as the 'child benefit extension period'.

  The amounts for your children vary according to their ages.

- ☐ **Premiums** are additional amounts paid to particular groups of people. There are premiums for families with children; pensioners; lone parents; disabled people; carers; and disabled children. The pensioner and disability premiums are all paid at either a single or a couple rate. Appendix 3 gives more details about who can get each premium.

- ☐ **'Housing costs'** that can be paid as part of your income support include:
  - **mortgage interest payments.** Usually the Benefits Agency can only pay the interest on a mortgage or loan taken out to buy the home (including a second mortgage). The loan does not have to be secured

on the property. However, they can pay the interest on a new mortgage which is paying off an earlier one on the same property, provided the earlier one qualified. There are a number of common situations in which less than the whole amount of the interest will be paid (see page 37). Income support does not cover the capital repayments, or the insurance premiums for an endowment mortgage. (For this reason, it may be worth trying to change from an endowment mortgage, but get advice first from one of the agencies listed in Appendix 7);

- **interest on loans for repairs and improvements**. To qualify, loans do not have to be secured on the house. They must, however, be for 'major repairs necessary to maintain the fabric of the dwelling', as well as for the following improvements:
  - putting in bathroom fixtures – for example, a washbasin, bath, shower or toilet;
  - damp-proofing;
  - providing or improving ventilation or natural light;
  - providing or improving drainage facilities;
  - putting in electric lighting and sockets;
  - putting in heating, including central heating;
  - putting in storage facilities for fuel and refuse;
  - improving the structural condition of the home;
  - improving facilities for storing, preparing and cooking food;
  - insulation;
  - other improvements which are reasonable in the circumstances. This means reasonable in *your* particular circumstances.

  Interest on loans to pay service charges (see below) covering repairs and improvements can also be paid;

- **other secured loans**. Separated partners can sometimes get interest paid on other loans (for example, for a car), if they are secured on the home. The loan must have been acquired by your partner either solely or jointly with you, your partner must have left and cannot or will not pay the interest, and you must have to pay it to keep your home. It does not matter whether or not you were married. There is a similar rule if your partner has died;

- **ground rent**. This is included if you have a long lease of more than 21 years (or 'feu duty' in Scotland) ;

- **some service charges** – eg, for buildings insurance, management, and maintenance and cleaning of common areas. The reason you have to pay the charges must be connected with your occupation of the home –

for example, under the terms of a lease. The fact that, for example, you have to insure the home under your mortgage does not make it a service charge. But insurance payments under a *lease* are covered.

In some circumstances, if you are liable to pay housing costs on two homes at the same time, it may be possible to have both amounts included in your income support. This could be if you have left your old home because of the fear of domestic violence, or because you are moving house and are liable to pay on both homes for a short period, or if your partner is a student or on a government training course, and has to live away from home. Also, if you have a large family and you yourself therefore live in two properties, you can try to argue that they are really both part of one home so that you should, for example, get interest on loans on both. You may need to get advice about this from one of the organisations listed in Appendix 7.

Example

This example shows how the applicable amount is calculated.

Ms Francis is a 35-year-old lone parent with three children of twelve, ten and six. Her mortgage interest payments are £1,906 per year. She has been on income support for six months. Her applicable amount based on April 1994 rates (see Appendix 3) is:

personal allowances		£ p
	for herself	45.70
	for her children	
	6-year-old	15.65
	10-year-old	15.65
	12-year-old	23.00
premiums		
	family	10.05
	lone parent	5.10
housing costs		
	mortgage interest (1/52 of yearly figure)	36.65

The total of the allowances, premiums, and housing costs is £151.80 per week, which is the level of Ms Francis' needs. If her income is less than this figure, the difference will be made up by income support.

Your income and capital

Your income consists of the money you have coming in each week and any assumed income from your savings. The Benefits Agency will not necessarily take all your income into account in full. The main rules are set out here.

- ☐ **Benefits** usually count in full as part of your income – for example, child benefit and invalidity benefit. The main exceptions are attendance allowance, disability living allowance and council tax benefit, which are ignored completely.

- ☐ **Maintenance payments** for yourself and your children count in full as part of your income. No distinction is made between maintenance orders paid 'to' or 'for' a child – they all count. A lump-sum payment of maintenance can lead to you losing your benefit completely for a time. If your ex-partner pays money to a 'third party' on your behalf – for example, pays your mortgage capital payments to the building society, or buys some other item that benefit is not intended to cover – then this may be ignored by the Benefits Agency if it would be reasonable to do so. The agencies mentioned in Appendix 7 should be able to give you advice about this.

- ☐ **Earnings** from part-time work are not counted in full. The Benefits Agency will deduct any tax, national insurance, and half of any pension scheme contributions that you pay. Then they will also deduct:
  - £15 for people getting the lone parent, disability or carer premium (and in some cases the higher pensioner premium as well). See Appendix 3 for information about premiums; *or*
  - £15 for a couple, both under 60, who have been on income support for two years, where neither has been in full-time work or education for more than eight weeks during that period; *or*
  - £15 in certain other cases (for part-time firefighters, auxiliary coastguards, lifeboat volunteers, and territorial or reserve forces); *or*
  - £5 from the earnings of anyone else.

  If your children have any earnings – for example, from a paper round – these are ignored (unless the earnings are from a full-time job after they have left school and while you are claiming benefit for them, in which case at least £5 or £15, and sometimes more, is ignored).

- ☐ **Income from a mortgage payment protection plan** (see page 61) will be ignored if it is covering part of a mortgage or loan which the Benefits Agency will not pay – eg, capital repayments, or 50 per cent of the interest payments for the first 16 weeks (see page 40).

- ☐ **Tenants**: if you let a room and do not provide meals, you will be treated by the local Benefits Agency as having a tenant. Any rent you receive from the tenant is taken into account, apart from the first £4. An extra £8.60 is ignored if the rent they pay you includes heating. For the rules about income from lodgers, see page 45.
- ☐ **Income from capital** is usually ignored. However, if you save the income from your savings, it will eventually be counted as part of the savings.
- ☐ **Savings** and other capital up to £3,000 are ignored completely. Above this level, until they reach £8,000, your savings are assumed to give you an income of £1 for each £250, or part of £250, that you have over £3,000. This is known as **tariff income**. However, some capital or assets which would take your savings over £3,000 are ignored. See Appendix 4 for more details on what capital is ignored.

Example

This example shows how income and income support are calculated (based on April 1994 rates).

Ms Francis, a lone parent, gets child benefit for her three children (£26.70 per week) plus one parent benefit (£6.15 per week). She has maintenance of £18 per week and works part-time, with net earnings of £30 per week. She has savings of £3,400. Her income will be assessed as follows:

Child benefit (counts in full)	£26.70
One parent benefit (counts in full)	£6.15
Maintenance (counts in full)	£18.00
Earnings (£15 disregarded for a single parent)	£15.00
Tariff income from savings over £3,000	£2.00
Total income	**£67.85**

Once you know your applicable amount and your income, you can work out how much income support you are entitled to. In the case of Ms Hunter, this is:

Her applicable amount (see page 33)	£151.80
Less her income	£67.85
Her income support is	£83.95

All of her council tax will be paid for her by the local authority (see Chapter four).

INCOME SUPPORT AND YOUR MORTGAGE INTEREST

'**Housing costs**' is the term used to describe payments relating to your home which the Benefits Agency pays as part of your income support (see page 31). One type of housing cost is mortgage interest. In this section, we use the term 'mortgage interest' to mean interest on a secured loan to buy a share in your home (and not interest on any other sort of secured loan).

Are you liable to pay?

The basic rule is that only people who are *legally* liable for the mortgage repayments can be paid housing costs with their income support. Normally, of course, this is not a problem – if you are not liable for something you do not need benefit to pay it.

However, there are occasions when you will need to make payments even though you are not liable to do so. The obvious example is where your partner was liable but s/he has now left and is not keeping up the payments. If payments are not made, you risk being evicted. There is a special rule which says that, if the person liable to make payments is not doing so and you need to do so to keep the home, housing costs can be paid to you *either* if you and the liable person used to be partners *or* if it is reasonable to treat you as being liable.

Tell the Benefits Agency the position. You may find that, as a result of the non-payment, you were entitled to income support for a period before you claimed it. If so, you may be able to get a back payment of benefit to cover that earlier period. You could also try this to help clear the arrears. You should get advice from an advice agency (see Appendix 7).

There is another exception to the basic rule. If you share the mortgage costs with someone in your household (other than your partner or a close relative), you can sometimes get the costs paid as part of your income support, even though you are not legally liable to pay them. Again, get advice.

Other points to note

Housing costs can be paid for mortgage interest to buy freehold or leasehold property. If you already own the leasehold, they can be paid on a loan to buy the freehold. They can also be paid if you buy out your former partner (but see page 37). The payments must be to someone not in your household – but this could include your partner's trustee in bankruptcy, even though you and your partner had been co-owners before the bankruptcy.

The home need not be built when you get the loan. Indeed, if you build it yourself, you can charge something for your labour and get interest on this sum paid.

If you have a 'low-start' mortgage (see page 6), under which you do not have to pay all (or any) of the interest for at least two years, you can get housing costs for the accumulated interest you have to pay after the period of grace.

If your income support applicable amount includes housing costs for either mortgage interest or interest on a loan for repairs and improvements, the Benefits Agency will usually pay part of your income support direct to your lender. Where the 'mortgage interest direct' scheme applies, the Agency has no discretion in the matter, even if you don't want the money paid to your lender.

However, this will not be done if:

☐ you are subject to the 50 per cent reduction in mortgage interest for the first 16 weeks (see page 40). The scheme will then apply as soon as you become eligible for 100 per cent mortgage interest;

☐ your loan is with a lender who is not covered by the scheme or has opted out of it. This is likely to apply if your loan is with a foreign bank or in some cases a local authority.

The Benefits Agency will normally pay over the money every four weeks in arrears. If your income support does not meet your mortgage interest in full, you will have to make arrangements yourself to pay the difference to the lender.

If the interest rate comes down but the Benefits Agency continues to pay your lender at the old rate, the Benefits Agency should recover the over-payment from the lender, not by making deductions from your benefit. If they try to reclaim it from you, contact an advice agency (see Appendix 7).

WHEN YOU RECEIVE LESS THAN YOUR FULL HOUSING COSTS

In most cases, your mortgage interest will be included in full as part of your housing costs. However, you will not always get the full amount. In addition, you may not get *any* housing costs paid if you were already on income support when you took out a new loan.

New or increased loans

Since 2 May 1994, it has not generally been possible to get benefit for mortgage loans which are taken out while you, or your partner, are eligible for income support, if this has the effect of increasing the housing costs you get. The rule applies to existing mortgage loans which you increase as well as to new ones. And, if you or your partner come off income support and claim again within 26 weeks, the rule applies to loans taken out during the intervening period.

There are a number of **exceptions to the general rule** which apply if:

- ☐ you have been renting and getting housing benefit and you then buy a home. It need not be the place you were renting. However, you will not get more than the amount of housing benefit, and any other housing costs you had been getting. If your eligible housing costs later increase, so will your benefit. Note that there is an overlap between this exception and the rule which applies if you buy the place you had been renting (see page 43);

- ☐ you take out or increase a loan to adapt your home for a disabled person, or to buy a home which is more suited to her/his needs than your present home. A 'disabled person' is someone who is getting a disability premium, a disabled child premium, an enhanced pensioner premium or a higher pensioner premium (see Appendix 3), or who would get one of these premiums if s/he was eligible for income support;

- ☐ you have a boy and a girl both aged 10 or over and you buy another home so that they can have separate bedrooms;

- ☐ you have been getting housing costs paid for things like ground rent or service charges and you then buy another 'interest' in your home (for example, the freehold). To begin with, you will only get the amount you had been getting for those other costs (though it can go up if your housing costs as a whole later increase);

- ☐ you take out a loan to pay service charges for repairs and improvements to your home (see page 32 for the meaning of 'service charges').

In addition, the DSS says the rule should not apply to loans for repairs and improvements. The 'repairs and improvements' which qualify are set out on page 32, but note that, for this purpose, instead of the final category, there is a category for work which creates separate bedrooms for a boy and girl both aged ten or over.

Although the wording of the relevant provision is unclear, it seems that the rule will not stop you getting housing costs paid on a second home in those limited circumstances where this is otherwise possible (see page 33). Increases in interest payments will not be caught either. Nor will arrears of interest which have, for example, built up during the first 16 weeks of a claim (see page 40) or with a low-start mortgage (see page 6).

It seems that the rule *is* intended to apply if, following divorce or separation, you buy out your former partner's share – you will not get the mortgage interest paid in relation to that share. Similarly, if you take out a loan, or increase an existing loan, to buy a new home after separation, the rule will in principle apply. However, the DSS has said that its intention is that, where couples on income support separate, each should be entitled to housing costs up to the amount they got when they were together. So, for example, if you were getting housing costs paid on a mortgage of £50,000 when you were together, you should each be entitled to housing costs on a mortgage of up to £50,000 when you separate.

The DSS has also said that the new rules will not prevent you getting housing costs for non-housing loans, where this is possible (see page 32).

More generally, it is very important to bear in mind that the rule is aimed at people who incur housing costs for mortgage interest or loans for repairs and improvements for the first time while already on income support, or who increase mortgage interest costs while on income support. It will not matter if you *replace* one loan with another (for example, if you move), as long as the replacement loan is no larger than the previous one. In addition, housing costs on loans which you incurred *before* you or your partner claimed income support will be covered (subject to the 26-week rule mentioned above and the other rules described below).

The new rules are not very clear, and it is important that you get advice from one of the agencies listed in Appendix 7.

Loans over £125,000

Since August 1993, the government has put a limit on the size of loans which qualify for income support housing costs. Initially, the limit was £150,000, but since 11 April 1994, it has been reduced to £125,000. This applies to mortgage interest, but loans on repairs and improvements have to be taken into account when calculating whether you have gone over the limit. If your loan(s) is more than £125,000, interest up to that figure will be paid but not above it.

Exemptions from the rule

- ☐ Sometimes you can get interest paid on two homes if you are liable to make payments on both (see page 33). In this case, housing costs up to £125,000 can be paid for each;
- ☐ If a loan is taken out to adapt a home for **a disabled person**, the £125,000 limit does not apply. A 'disabled person' is someone who is getting a

disability premium, a disabled child premium, an enhanced pensioner premium or a higher pensioner premium (see Appendix 4) or is a 'non-dependant' (see page 41) who would be getting such a premium if s/he were entitled to income support;

- [ ] If you have been **entitled to income support since before 11 April 1994**, the limit will not apply to a loan you already had at that date, as long as you have not increased it since. And, if you have been entitled to income support since before 2 August 1993, the £150,000 limit will not apply either. Sometimes, periods of up to eight weeks when you were not entitled to income support can be ignored.

This restriction applies immediately you go on income support, so that it applies at the same time as the 50 per cent rule (see below).

The first 16 weeks on benefit

You will usually only get the full amount of your mortgage or loan interest included in your income support during the first 16 weeks of your claim if you, or your partner, are aged 60 or more. If you, and your partner, are under 60 the Benefits Agency will only pay 50 per cent of your interest payments for the first 16 weeks. After that, they will pay the full amount. This rule will not affect you if:

- [ ] you were getting income support before, and you have only interrupted your claim by less than eight weeks – for example, you might have taken a temporary job; *or*

- [ ] you have started claiming as a couple within the last eight weeks, and your new partner had been getting income support; *or*

- [ ] you have separated from your partner within the last eight weeks, and s/he had been claiming income support for you.

In any of these circumstances, the period during which you or your partner were previously getting income support will count towards the 16 weeks.

If you are affected by this rule, and you spend more than 16 weeks on benefit, you will qualify for additional benefit to meet the interest due on arrears which have built up as a result of the Benefits Agency only meeting 50 per cent of your interest payments.

As a result of this rule, you may claim income support but not qualify, whereas you would have done so if mortgage interest payments had counted in full as part of your applicable amount. In these circumstances, see page 44 for what to do for the first 16 weeks. After 16 weeks, make a second claim for income support and your applicable amount should then include your mortgage interest in full. It is important that you make the first claim, even though you do not expect to qualify, to get the 16 weeks taken into account.

Other people sharing your home (non-dependants)

A 'non-dependant' is someone who lives with you but is not your partner or dependent child and who pays no rent. The most common type of non-dependant is a grown up child or other relative who lives in your home (and perhaps gives you something towards their keep). Non-dependants are expected to contribute towards your housing costs, but a deduction from your housing costs is made whether or not they do. The amount of contribution or whether any is expected at all is dependent on the person's age and whether or not s/he is in work.

The Benefits Agency will therefore make the following deductions from the weekly amount you would otherwise get for your housing costs, and ignore any income that you actually receive from the non-dependant. For the rules about boarders and tenants, see page 45. The deductions for non-dependants are:

Non-dependants aged 18 or over and in full-time work (16 hours or more a week) with a weekly gross income of

less than £72	£ 5.00
between £72 and £107.99	£9.00
between £108 and £138.99	£13.00
£139 or more	£25.00
Non-dependants aged 25 or over on income support	£5.00
Non-dependants aged 18 or over not in full-time work	£5.00

No deduction at all is made if you or your partner are blind, or getting attendance allowance, or the care component of disability living allowance. In addition, no deduction is made in the case of certain non-dependants – for example, people aged under 25 on income support and full-time students (including during the summer vacation unless they work then).

Also, only one deduction will be made where you have a couple living with you. The higher appropriate deduction will be made if their circumstances differ.

A deduction is not made unless the non-dependant is living in your home, that is, sharing your home. If you provide them with self-contained accommodation they should not be counted as non-dependants.

Shared ownership

Income support will not meet all your housing costs if you are buying under a 'shared ownership' arrangement (see page 7). This is because your payments are both for the part you are buying on mortgage and for the element you are renting. You are entitled to income support to meet the interest element of the mortgage payments, but for help with the rental payments you will need to claim housing benefit (see page 24).

'Excessive' interest payments

The Benefits Agency can refuse to pay the whole of your mortgage interest (or other housing costs) if they think it is too much. However, this happens rarely. They can only do it if they think *either* your home (excluding any rooms you let or which are occupied by boarders) is unnecessarily large for you and your family, *or* the immediate area in which you live is unnecessarily expensive *or* the cost of the mortgage or other housing costs are unreasonably high when compared with the cost of suitable alternative accommodation in the area. But if it is not reasonable to expect you to move, the Benefits Agency must approve payment of your mortgage interest in full. Examples of when it would not be reasonable to expect you to move are where:

- [ ] you cannot sell your home; *or*
- [ ] there is no other suitable accommodation available to you; *or*
- [ ] there is little cheaper accommodation in the general area; *or*
- [ ] you would not be able to obtain another mortgage and, if you rented, the proceeds of sale from your present home would take you over the capital limit for housing benefit; *or*
- [ ] your personal circumstances – especially your age, state of health, employment prospects, and the effect of a change of school on your children (including any foster children) – would make it unreasonable to expect you to move; *or*
- [ ] the Benefits Agency told you before you moved that full interest would be paid.

In all cases of excessive interest, the Benefits Agency counts the whole of your mortgage interest as part of your housing costs for six months if you or your partner could afford the mortgage when it was taken on. Whether it was a wise decision is irrelevant. The interest may continue to be paid in full for a further six months after that, if you are doing your best to find cheaper accommodation. Only after that will the restriction apply, and even then you should be given advance warning that you should look around.

The rules which allow the Benefits Agency to reduce the amount of benefit which you receive towards the mortgage interest apply even if you are already having only 50 per cent of your interest payments met (see page 40). But, remember that the restriction will not apply for the first six months if you could afford the mortgage when you took it on, which would mean that the 50 per cent rule would apply to the *full* cost.

You use your home for business or other purposes

If a part of your house is used for purposes other than as a home for your family, the Benefits Agency may decide to limit your mortgage interest. If this happens, you should probably get advice from one of the organisations mentioned in Appendix 7. You will only be entitled to help with that proportion of the mortgage interest which relates to the part of the property you actually live in.

You have bought a property you previously rented

If, while receiving income support, you buy the property you used to rent *and* in which you previously had security of tenure – for example, you were a council tenant – the Benefits Agency will not necessarily pay your full housing costs. Instead, they will limit your housing costs to the amount of rent used to calculate housing benefit when you were a tenant. If, subsequently, your housing costs rise again, you will be allowed to include this increase as part of your housing requirements.

If the interest rate goes up, so will your housing costs – and they will not come down again even if the interest rate does (unless the amount of interest you are *actually* paying comes down below the increased housing costs you had been getting). For example, assume you had been getting £75 a week housing benefit and that, when you buy your house, your mortgage interest, at 10 per cent, is £100 per month: you will only get £75 housing costs. If the interest rate then rises by 1 per cent, the interest you will actually have to pay your lender is £110, an increase of £10. Your housing costs will also be increased by £10, to £85. Assume that the interest rate then comes down to 9 per cent, so that you are actually paying £90. In this case, your housing costs will remain at £85 and will only reduce if your actual interest payments come down below that figure.

Note that there is an overlap between this rule and one of the exceptions to the new rule that new or increased loans do not qualify if you are already getting income support (see page 37). You should get advice from one of the agencies in Appendix 7.

The restriction can only be lifted if there is a 'major change' in your family's circumstances which makes it more difficult for you to pay your housing costs – for example, you bought the house jointly with your working son who has now moved out or who has become unemployed. It may be possible to circumvent the restriction by coming off income support before you complete the purchase or by later coming off income support for a period of over eight weeks. However, before taking such a step you should consult one of the organisations mentioned in Appendix 7.

Your loan only partly qualifies for income support

Your help from income support towards housing costs will not be the full amount of mortgage interest where only part of the loan was used to purchase your home. For example, if the mortgage was taken out so that 75 per cent could be used to buy a house and 25 per cent to buy a car or clear other debts, you will only qualify for help towards the 75 per cent. Special rules apply if the loan was taken out solely or jointly by a partner from whom you are now separated or who has now died (see page 32).

You share the costs

If you share the mortgage costs with someone other than your partner, you will only get housing costs for the share you actually pay, even though, legally, you are liable for the whole sum.

Arrears and interest on arrears

You cannot normally get mortgage arrears paid. However, the Benefits Agency may call something 'arrears' which is not. For example, if you are allowed, under your mortgage agreement, to postpone interest payments, they are not 'arrears' and you can get housing costs for them when you do have to pay them. In addition, you may be able to backdate your income support claim to cover arrears of interest payments (see page 47).

Similarly, you cannot normally get housing costs for interest on arrears. However, you can, in certain circumstances with a low-start mortgage (see page 6), or if you are affected by the 16-week rule (see page 40).

HOW TO PAY UNMET INTEREST, MORTGAGE CAPITAL OR INSURANCE PREMIUMS

These are some suggestions for how you can try to meet any part of your housing costs not being paid by the Benefits Agency. However, if the problem is that your lender is refusing to accept interest only payments, it is worth negotiating on this point, before trying to raise the cash (see Chapter five for suggestions on how to negotiate).

Get a part-time job

A small amount of your earnings will be ignored by the Benefits Agency when they work out your benefit (see page 34), so you could put this money towards the unmet part of your mortgage.

Childminding

There are special rules for someone who is on benefit and working as a childminder. This is because the Benefits Agency will ignore two-thirds of the money you make and only count a third as earnings and they will not treat you as being in full-time work even if you mind children for more than 16 hours each week (in your home).

Take in a boarder

A person will be treated as a boarder (or lodger) if you take them in on a commercial basis and the charge you make covers meals. The first £20 of the payments you receive will not affect your income support.

After that only half of the balance is treated as income and taken into account when calculating your benefit. It may be worth working out roughly how much you would have to spend on providing board and lodging, so you know whether it will be worth your while having a boarder. You may find it helpful to read the government leaflet on boarders, *Want to Rent a Room?*, which you could get from the Department of the Environment (see Appendix 9) or from one of the organisations mentioned in Appendix 7. See also the special note overleaf.

Take in a tenant

You would probably be taking in a 'tenant' if you were to provide someone with their own room or self-contained part of your home without providing them with meals or services such as room-cleaning. If you provided meals and/or services they would probably be your lodger rather than your tenant (see above). You might find a tenant either by advertising for one yourself in a newspaper or newsagent's shop or through an accommodation agency.

You are normally free to charge what you like at the outset if they first become your tenant after January 1989 and it is a good idea to make some sort of written tenancy agreement which sets out the details of the arrangement. The government leaflet, *Letting Rooms in Your Home* (which you can also get from the Department of the Environment or an advice agency) outlines the implications of taking in a tenant. If you and the tenant will be sharing parts of your home – for example, the use of the bathroom – it is very unlikely that the tenant would have the right to stay on after the arrangement came to an end although, of course, you should never try to physically throw someone out. If you and your tenant are in dispute, take advice from one of the organisations in Appendix 7.

If you are claiming income support and have a tenant, all but £4 of what you charge will be deducted from your benefit (although you are allowed to keep an extra £8.60 if the charge you make includes heating). You may find that, if you are on benefit, you would be better off financially by taking a boarder (see page 45) instead of a tenant.

A special note if you take a tenant or a boarder

- **Your local Benefits Agency office:** you have to let your office know of any changes in your circumstances. You should write to the Benefits Agency explaining what new arrangements you have made and, if you want them to treat the new person as a boarder, it is important that you say that you are providing cooked meals. It is vital that you do this if you are a lone parent and offer a room to someone of the opposite sex. A written statement from you at the office should pre-empt any problems over neighbours or others telling the office that you and your boarder are 'cohabiting'. Otherwise you could risk losing your benefit (see page 29). Keep a copy of your letter.

- **Your lender:** your mortgage agreement will probably state that you must not let a room or take in a boarder. If you have already let a room and there are no problems with the mortgage, the chances are that your lender will not bother about what you are doing. However, if you are trying to negotiate a change in your mortgage with your lender and they discover that you are letting a room, they may be unwilling to help you. If this happens you should seek advice from one of the agencies listed in Appendix 7, or you could look at some of the other ways of raising extra cash.

- **Your boarder/tenant:** don't forget that you are offering someone a home even if it is in your own house or flat. Depending on the arrangements between you, they could have some limited rights in that home under laws which deal with landlords and tenants. In particular, you might be responsible for repairs or find it difficult to make your boarder/tenant leave immediately if things don't work out. Ask for advice on this from one of the agencies listed in Appendix 7 before you take anyone in.

Help from a friend, relative or charity

If you have a friend, relative or charity prepared to pay the unmet mortgage interest or mortgage capital or insurance premium for you, this amount will not reduce your weekly benefit, because it is paying for something which your income support is not meant to cover. However, the friend or relative must not be your ex-partner, or the other parent of your children. Any money from her/him counts in full as maintenance unless s/he pays the money direct to the lender, in which case the Benefits Agency should ignore it if it is unreasonable to count it.

Benefit arrears and backdating

Another way to raise money to pay your housing costs, and other bills, is to check whether or not you are owed arrears of benefit. First, check your current weekly benefit for all the different elements described on pages 31-35. You may not be getting them all or the amount you are receiving may be wrong (check the figures in Appendix 3). If you find something is wrong or missing, write and ask that it be put right and your arrears paid. If it was the Benefits Agency office that made a mistake about the amount of your income support, the arrears can be backdated indefinitely. You should get advice from one of the agencies in Appendix 7. If you are getting less because, for example, you failed to report something, your arrears can only be backdated for a maximum of one year. If you were on supplementary benefit before April 1988, you may have been underpaid then. An advice centre may be able to check this for you.

The second way to get arrears is to ask for your whole claim for income support to be backdated for up to 12 months. You can do this if you find that you could have qualified for benefit before the date on which you actually claimed. You will be able to get benefit backdated in this way if, for the whole of the period before you claimed, you had 'good cause' for not doing so. Deciding whether you have 'good cause' involves looking at why you did not claim earlier (see page 29 on the meaning of 'good cause').

Contact one of the agencies listed in Appendix 7 for advice about backdating of benefit.

CHALLENGING DECISIONS ABOUT YOUR INCOME SUPPORT

If the local Benefits Agency office refuses to give you what you ask for, it is always worth considering whether to appeal to an independent tribunal.

You can get help from the organisations listed in Appendix 7.

You appeal by writing to the Benefits Agency office saying that you wish to appeal against the decision. It is usually best to give a full explanation of why you disagree with the decision. In some cases, this may lead to the decision being changed without your having to go to the tribunal. You have three months from the date of the Benefits Agency's decision in which to appeal. This period can be extended if you can show good reason why you did not appeal in time.

It is important that you go to the hearing yourself and that, if possible, you get help in preparing and presenting your case. If you cannot attend the tribunal for whatever reason, or need more time to prepare, write to the clerk to the tribunal and ask for an adjournment.

OTHER RELATED BENEFITS

Housing benefit

See page 24. If you are claiming income support from the Benefits Agency, you can claim housing benefit at the same time.

Council tax benefit

Being entitled to income support (or having an income almost low enough to get income support) means that you will qualify for council tax benefit. There is a claim form for this inside the income support claim which you return to the Benefits Agency. You could also apply directly to the local authority on its own application form. You may be entitled to council tax benefit if you are legally liable to pay council tax.

For more about council tax benefit, see Chapter 4.

Health, education and other benefits and grants

Income support gives automatic entitlement to a range of health and education benefits. For education benefits, see page 24. The health benefits that you and your family will be entitled to are:

- ☐ free prescriptions;

- ☐ free dental treatment;

- ☐ free sight tests and 'full-value' vouchers for glasses or contact lenses;

- ☐ free milk tokens for expectant mothers and children under five;

- free vitamins for expectant and nursing mothers (ie, those breastfeeding a child under 30 weeks' old) and children under five;
- refunds of hospital fares for treatment;
- free school meals.

See page 25 for the entitlement of children to health benefits.

In addition, if you are getting income support, you can apply for the local authority and Home Energy Efficiency Scheme grants discussed in Chapter seven.

THE SOCIAL FUND SCHEME

The social fund is part of the social security system run by the Benefits Agency. It has two parts. There is one part under which you can ask for financial help but you have no right to it. This is called the **discretionary social fund**. It can provide grants and loans and is described on pages 50-51. The other part provides lump sums to meet some of the costs of maternity needs, funeral expenses and heating costs in very cold weather. You can apply for these payments through the local social security office as follows:

- **maternity expenses:** you qualify for a lump sum of £100 if you or a member of your family are expecting a baby within the next 11 weeks (or have had one within the last three months) and you or your partner are receiving income support (see page 28), family credit (see page 14), or disability working allowance (see page 19).

- **funeral expenses:** you may qualify for a lump-sum payment to help meet basic funeral costs if you take responsibility for a funeral and you or your partner are receiving council tax benefit (see Chapter four), family credit (see page 14) or income support (see page 28), housing benefit (see page 24), disability working allowance (see page 19), and you claim within three months of the funeral.

- **cold weather grants:** you qualify for a grant of £7 per week during spells of very cold weather (an average of 0° Celsius forecast or recorded for seven consecutive days) if you are receiving income support (see page 28) and either have a child under five or are receiving a premium as a pensioner or disabled person or for a disabled child (see page 31). There is no need to claim, however, as the Benefits Agency should send you payment automatically.

For maternity expenses and funeral expenses, you will get a reduced amount if you have more than £500 savings or other capital. For every £1 of savings over £500 (£1,000 if you, or your partner, are 60 or over) you will get £1 less in grant. In addition, certain sums are deducted from a funeral payment – for example, assets of the deceased which are available without probate being granted.

Having worked out whether you qualify for these sorts of grants, read on to see if you can get help from the discretionary social fund.

Discretionary social fund

Most payments from the social fund are discretionary. Normally you do not have a right to receive a payment (the only exceptions are payments for funerals, maternity needs, and cold weather – see above). The fund has a limited budget, so if it runs out during the year, no more payments can be made. If you are refused a payment from the social fund, there is no independent right of appeal, although you can ask for an internal 'review' of the decision, and then a further review by a social fund inspector. Social fund officers work from local Benefits Agency offices.

Most payments made by the social fund will be loans that have to be repaid out of weekly benefit. However, some are grants. These are called **community care grants**.

Community care grants

You generally have to be on income support to apply for a community care grant, and the law says that you can get one in order to:

☐ help ease exceptional pressures on you and your family;

☐ help you re-establish yourself in the community after a period in institutional or residential care;

☐ enable you to remain living in the community, rather than going into institutional or residential care;

☐ help meet certain travel expenses.

Since all community care grant decisions are at the discretion of the social fund officer, there are few rules about when you should get a community care grant, and for what. There are a number of items for which you *cannot* get a community care grant – for example, you cannot get a community care grant for most repairs and improvements and other 'housing costs' such as mortgage payments, water rates and service charges. The same applies to budgeting and crisis loans (see below). In all three cases, however, you can get a payment for *minor* repairs. It may be worth arguing that an item of repair is only minor.

The rules say that, when deciding whether to make a payment, the social fund officer should take account of any other resources that you have available to meet the need. If they do decide to make a payment, the amount will be reduced if you have savings over £500 (£1,000 if you or your partner are over 60).

Loans

The social fund also makes **budgeting loans** to people who have been on income support for six months. These are intended to cover a variety of one-off needs that are difficult to budget for out of weekly benefit. These loans may be available for a wide range of things, including furniture, removal charges, redecoration, etc. There are also **crisis loans** for meeting needs in an emergency, or after a disaster. You do not need to be on income support to get a crisis loan. Emergencies might include loss of money, or when you are waiting for your first benefit payment after your initial claim. As with community care grants, there are a number of items for which you cannot get a budgeting or crisis loan.

Although these loans are interest-free, they are recovered by deductions from weekly benefit at what may be a relatively high weekly rate. They can also be recovered from your partner's benefit in certain circumstances.

OTHER BENEFITS

If you have paid sufficient national insurance contributions, you may be entitled to various other benefits – such as unemployment benefit or sickness benefit – regardless of your other income or savings. And, if you are disabled or care for a disabled person, there are a number of benefits to which you may be entitled even if you have not paid national insurance contributions. You can get child benefit if you have a child under 16, or under 19 if s/he is in full-time secondary education, living with you, and in certain other circumstances too. Depending on your means, you can get income support on top of all these benefits.

You should get advice from one of the organisations listed in Appendix 7, and see CPAG's *Rights Guide to Non-Means-Tested Benefits* (see Appendix 9).

CHAPTER FOUR

Council tax and council tax benefit

Council tax replaced the community charge (poll tax) in April 1993. Council tax benefit was introduced at the same time. There are two forms of council tax benefit, main council tax benefit and alternative maximum council tax benefit (usually known as second adult rebate). You do not have to be getting any other state benefit to qualify.

It is useful to have a basic understanding of how council tax works. Do not necessarily assume that the local authority has got your bill right. You may, in fact, be entitled to a reduction of your council tax bill even without claiming council tax benefit.

The rules for both council tax and council tax benefit are fairly complicated. If you are in any doubt about your position, get advice from one of the agencies listed in Appendix 7. See also the SHAC/CIH *Guide to Housing Benefit and Council Tax Benefit* and CPAG's *Council Tax Handbook* (Appendix 9).

COUNCIL TAX

Council tax is a tax on residential properties ('dwellings'). Some dwellings are exempt from the tax. A dwelling may be exempt *indefinitely* – for example, if it has been left unoccupied by a former resident because s/he is in hospital or if all the residents are students. Or it may be exempt *for up to six months* – for example, if the dwelling is unoccupied and is part of the estate of someone who has died.

How much are you liable to pay?

Local authorities set the overall amount of council tax for their area. The amount which you have to pay depends on the valuation band into which your dwelling has been put. There are eight bands, A-H. A is the lowest band and H the highest. Which band your dwelling falls into depends on its value in April 1991, as set by district valuers. That was not necessarily its open market sale value: valuers had to make certain assumptions – for example, that your dwelling was in reasonable repair.

However, there are a number of ways in which **your bill could be reduced**:

- [ ] **If you or someone who lives in your dwelling as their only or main home is substantially and permanently disabled**, you pay tax appropriate for the band below the one in which the dwelling actually is. So, if the dwelling, based on its value in April 1991, is in band D, you pay tax on the lower band C rate. Note that you do not have to be disabled yourself, as long as someone in the dwelling is. The dwelling must have certain facilities which are essential, or at least very important, for the disabled person – for example, a second bathroom or kitchen with appropriate facilities. It is not necessary that special adaptations have been carried out.

- [ ] **You may be eligible for a discount**. Council tax is based on the assumption that there are two adults living in the dwelling. If, in fact, you live alone, your bill will be reduced by at least 25 per cent.

- [ ] Some people who live in your dwelling may be ignored for council tax purposes if they have **status discount**. There is a long list of people with status discount – for example, many students, people under 25 on Youth Training Schemes, and carers providing care for at least 35 hours a week and living with the person needing care. So, if you live with a person with status discount and with no one else, you are treated as living alone and your bill will therefore be reduced.

  It is possible that all the residents of a dwelling will have status discount. In this case, the total liability will be for only 50 per cent of the normal bill. Note that people with status discount can still be *liable for the bill* (see below). Note also that the presence of someone with status discount will *not* reduce the bill if there are at least two other residents not entitled to status discount.

  If the dwelling is empty but you are liable to pay tax on it, your bill is reduced by 50 per cent. However, in Wales, local authorities can take away this discount, or only give a 25 per cent discount, for some second homes.

- [ ] **You may be eligible for a transitional reduction**. This was introduced in April 1993 by the government to cushion the blow for households who would otherwise have had to pay much more in council tax than they had to pay in community charge. A limit is put on the increased tax a household has to pay as a result of the changeover. It will generally apply until April 1995, although for some dwellings it only applied until April 1994. It attaches to the property rather than to the people who lived there in April 1993. So, if you moved in after April 1993, you may benefit from the transitional reduction already on the dwelling.

Who is liable to pay?

Liability for council tax rests with **residents** or **owners**.

Residents

A 'resident' is someone who is aged 18 or over and who lives in the dwelling as their only or main home. If there is **more than one resident,** who is liable depends on the basis on which they live in the dwelling. The liable person is the person who falls into the first category you come to as you go down this list:

- ☐ an owner-occupier;
- ☐ a tenant;
- ☐ a statutory or secure tenant;
- ☐ a licensee in England and Wales or a sub-tenant in Scotland;
- ☐ any other resident (eg, a squatter in England and Wales).

If there is more than one person in any of these categories, they are generally all **jointly and severally liable**. What this means is that if, for example, there are two tenants (ie, two people in the same category) and no owner-occupier, the local authority can look to either of them for payment of the whole bill. In addition, married or unmarried members of a heterosexual couple are jointly and severally liable if their partner falls within the relevant category. For example, if your partner owns the freehold, you will be liable with her/him if you both live in the dwelling. Gay and lesbian couples will not be jointly and severally liable unless they are both otherwise owner-occupiers, tenants and so forth.

There is an exception to the general rule about joint and several liability in the case of **severely mentally impaired people**. A severely mentally impaired person is only liable if all the other liable people are also severely mentally impaired, or if there is no other liable person. You are severely mentally impaired if you have a 'severe impairment of intelligence and social functioning (however caused) which appears to be permanent'.

Note that the local authority does not have to put the names of all jointly and severally liable people on the bill.

Owners

An 'owner' in England and Wales is someone who is a freeholder or a leaseholder (including someone with a sub-lease of six months or more), or in Scotland a heritable proprietor. Owners who do not live in the dwelling are liable if there are no residents (as defined above), or if the property has been built or adapted for multiple occupation (ie, where each resident *either* occupies only part of the dwelling *or* is only liable to pay rent on part of the dwelling).

The same rules about joint and several liability apply to owners as to residents.

The question of liability is very important for council tax benefit, because only liable people are eligible for council tax benefit.

Payment of council tax

You can pay your bill in ten monthly instalments or by lump sum. Local authorities have the power to give discounts for payments made by lump sum. They can also give discounts for 'non-cash' payments (eg, direct debit). Check with your local authority whether they give discounts.

In addition, local authorities can enter into a special arrangement with you for payment. This could prove very useful if you have temporary financial difficulties. The arrangement can be entered into even after the bill has been sent to you.

Bills are issued at the beginning of the financial year (April) and are for the full year. However, your circumstances may change during the year (or you may, of course, move). You should let the local authority know about any changes which might affect the size of the bill. For example, your partner may have left, so that you may well be entitled to a discount (see page 53). Your bill will be recalculated from the time of the change.

COUNCIL TAX BENEFIT

As mentioned at the start of this chapter, there are two sorts of council tax benefit: main council tax benefit and second adult rebate. You are entitled to whichever is the more generous in your circumstances. The local authority should work this out. You do not have to specify which one you want.

Main council tax benefit: the calculation

Benefit is based on your liability *after* the various reductions set out above.

Main council tax benefit is a means-tested benefit. In other words, whether you are eligible depends on your income and capital.

If you are getting income support, you will get maximum council tax benefit, which means that you will not have to pay any council tax on your share unless you have 'non-dependants' living with you (see below).

If you are not getting income support, you have to go through a number of steps:

Step 1: Check that your capital is no more than £16,000 (see Appendix 4 for further information about how capital is calculated).

Step 2: Work out your income. Some forms of income can be ignored and various deductions can be made as well. The rules are similar to family credit (see page 14) and income support (see page 28), but not identical. For more information see CPAG's *National Welfare Benefits Handbook* (listed in Appendix 9). In addition, the advice agencies mentioned in Appendix 7 will be able to help you. Note that, from October 1994, childcare costs of up to £40 can sometimes be deducted (see page 19).

Step 3: Work out your 'applicable amount' (ie, personal allowances and premiums). The rules for working this out are similar to income support (see Appendix 4), but the lone parent premium is £11.25 for council tax benefit.

Step 4: Compare the figures from Step 2 and Step 3. If your income is equal to, or less than, your applicable amount, you are entitled to maximum council tax benefit. If it is higher, go on to Step 5.

Step 5: Work out 20 per cent of the difference between your income and applicable amount (assuming your income is higher) and deduct it from your maximum council tax liability.

Step 6: Deduct any non-dependant deductions (see below).

The result is the weekly amount of benefit to which you are entitled.

Example
Janet is a 35-year-old lone parent. She has two children, Jamie aged 13 and Samantha aged 8. There are no non-dependants living with them. Janet has less than £3,000 in savings *(Step 1)*. Her net income which has to be taken into account is £130 per week *(Step 2)*. Her home is in band D. Full council tax for dwellings in band D is £600, but because Janet is the only adult her liability, before considering council tax benefit, is reduced by twenty five per cent, to £450. This works out as £1.23 a day, or £8.61 a week.

Her applicable amount *(Step 3)* is worked out as follows (at 1994/95 rates):

Her personal allowance	£ 45.70
Personal allowance for Jamie	£ 23.00
Personal allowance for Samantha	£ 15.65
Family premium	£ 10.05
Lone parent premium	£ 11.25
	£105.65

Janet's income (£130) is more than her applicable amount (£105.65) – by £24.35 *(Step 4)*. She is therefore not entitled to maximum council tax benefit and will have to pay some council tax. *Step 5:* 20 per cent of £24.35 is £4.87. To find out how much council tax benefit Janet is entitled to a week, you then deduct this sum from her maximum council tax liability of £8.61 a week, leaving £3.74. That is her weekly council tax benefit. In other words, she has to pay £4.87 instead of £8.61.

Non-dependant deductions

If someone other than your partner or dependent child lives with you on a non-commercial basis (ie, they do not pay rent to you), but they are not themselves jointly liable with you for the tax, deductions have to be made from your council tax benefit. This is because it is considered reasonable that they should contribute towards your council tax bill. It does not matter whether they actually do pay you something. The deductions are worked out as follows (at 1994/95 rates):

Circumstances of the non-dependant	*Deduction*
18 or over and in full-time work with a weekly gross income of	
£108 or more	£2.30
Up to £107.99	£1.15
Others aged 18 or over	£1.15

In certain circumstances, no non-dependant deductions are made – for example, if the non-dependant is on income support or is a full-time student, or if you or your partner are getting attendance allowance or the care component of disability living allowance.

Only one deduction is made for a non-dependant couple. Where the circumstances of each partner are different, the higher appropriate deduction is made. However, in deciding which level of deduction should be made for someone in full-time work, the joint income of a couple is always used – even if only one of them is a full-time worker.

Exceptional circumstances

You can be awarded more than the normal amount of main council tax benefit if the local authority considers that your circumstances are exceptional – you can get benefit up to one hundred per cent of your tax liability. Examples of exceptional circumstances might be if your heating costs are abnormally high or your living costs are high because of disability.

Second adult rebate: the calculation

You are eligible for a second adult rebate if you are liable for council tax, the presence of a second adult in the dwelling prevents you getting the discount you would otherwise get (see page 53) and s/he is considered too poor to compensate you for the loss of discount. The second adult must live with you on a non-commercial basis. **The following people are *not* counted as second adults:**

- ☐ someone with a status discount (see page 53);
- ☐ your heterosexual partner;
- ☐ someone else who is jointly liable with you for the council tax.

The rebate is based on the council tax liability for the dwelling *before* discounts are applied but *after* any disability and transitional reductions (see page 53). The amount of the rebate depends on the income of the *second adult*, as follows (at 1994/95 rates):

Income of the second adult	*Second adult rebate (per cent)*
Second adult (or all second adults) on income support	25
Second adult(s) total gross income:	
Up to £107.99 a week	15
£108-£138.99 a week	7.5
£139 a week or more	nil

Because it is the income of the second adult which has to be taken into account, you need to know what they earn. If they are not willing to tell you, they may be willing to tell the local authority instead, or you may be able to give the local authority an idea of what they are likely to earn because of their job. 'Income' in this context includes both earnings and non-earned income including most social security benefits, but it does not include attendance allowance and disability living allowance.

Note that, unlike main council tax benefit, the fact that you have savings of more than £16,000 does not mean that you cannot get second adult rebate.

Exceptional circumstances

If the local authority considers that your circumstances are exceptional (see page 58) it can give you a rebate up to the maximum 25 per cent even though the income of the second adult would otherwise mean you are entitled to less.

How to claim council tax benefit (main council benefit and second adult rebate)

Anyone who has to pay council tax can make a claim for council tax benefit. There are two ways to claim:

- ☐ If you make a claim for income support, you can claim council tax benefit at the same time, using form NHB1(CTB). Your local social security office will then pass the claim form to your local authority (in Scotland this is your regional council); or

- ☐ you can get a claim form from your local authority or your regional council.

You should claim as soon as possible. Payment can be backdated for up to a year if you can show 'good cause' for the delay in claiming (for example, because you did not realise you were jointly liable for the tax because your name was not on the bill). Get advice from an advice agency listed in Appendix 7 about this. You should inform the local authority of any change in your circumstances which may affect your entitlement to council tax benefit, or the amount of benefit – for example, if your earnings increase.

If you are jointly and severally liable for the bill (see page 54), you can only claim benefit on a share of it. For example, if you are sharing a house with two friends, your benefit is worked out on a one-third share. With main council tax benefit, the share is of the tax liability for the dwelling after deducting discounts and reductions (see page 53). With second adult rebate, the share is of the liability before discounts but after reductions. In either case, you can claim on behalf of your heterosexual partner. Note that, except where the only liable people are heterosexual partners, you might have to pay a larger share of the bill than you get benefit on. Indeed, the local authority might look to you for the whole bill, but you will still only get benefit on the relevant share. You can look to the other liable people to compensate you so that you are not out of pocket.

Challenging a decision

If you are unhappy with a decision about **council tax benefit** or **transitional reduction** you can ask your local authority to review it. If you are still unhappy, you can ask for a further review by a Council Tax Benefit Review Board, which is made up of councillors.

It is now too late to appeal against the **valuation band** into which the dwelling was put in April 1993. However, in certain circumstances it is possible to *make a proposal* that the banding should be changed for the future. For example, if you become liable for the tax on a particular dwelling for the first time, you can propose a different valuation within six months. Similarly, a proposal can be made within six months where a dwelling is first shown on the valuation list after April 1993, for example because it has just been built.

In addition, a valuation can be changed at any time if:

- the dwelling has significantly increased in value as a result of building works (for example, an extension) and has then been sold, or, in England and Wales only, has been let on a lease for seven years or more;

- the dwelling has significantly reduced in value because of demolition of part of it, a change in the locality (for example, a new road) or any adaptation to make it suitable for a physically disabled person.

If you think that the valuation band of your home should be altered, you should write to the listing officer or, in Scotland, the local assessor. Ask your local authority for the addresses. If you are unhappy with the outcome, the matter will be referred to a Valuation Tribunal, or, in Scotland, a Valuation Appeal Committee.

Note that a listing officer or assessor can also change the valuation if s/he thinks that the original valuation was wrong. However, the government has announced that, where an *undervaluation* has come to light as a result of the sale of neighbouring property, you will not face a bill for arrears of tax. The corrected valuation will only apply for the future. If there has been an *overvaluation* of your dwelling, you should get a backdated rebate.

If you are unhappy with a decision as to whether someone is or is not a **liable person**, or about **discounts** or **reductions** (except transitional reductions), or a decision that a dwelling is not **exempt**, you can appeal to a Valuation Tribunal or Valuation Appeal Committee. However, initially you should write to the local authority setting out your complaint.

OTHER BENEFITS AND GRANTS

If you get council tax benefit, you can apply for a social fund funeral payment (see page 49), a Home Energy Efficiency Scheme grant (see page 90) and a grant for 'minor works assistance' (see page 87).

CHAPTER FIVE

Cutting your mortgage costs

If you are not able to make the monthly payments to your lenders, you risk losing your home. Any lender of a mortgage or secured loan can apply to a court for an order to sell your home. You could lose your home unless you can show that you can, and will, manage in future.

If you are having difficulties with your payments, discuss this first with your lender. Your lender can help by looking at ways of rearranging your payments, either temporarily or permanently, to help you manage. *Do not stop paying.* It is better to pay what you can while, at the same time, looking at ways of cutting your costs.

This chapter explains how you can reduce your monthly mortgage costs by rearranging your loan(s) and also describes the best way to approach your lenders with your proposals. The following arrangements have all been reached by people having difficulties with their mortgages. However, you might well be told that your own proposals are not acceptable. *Do not let this put you off.* Most lenders, but especially building societies and local authorities, have such wide powers that they can accept almost any proposal they consider appropriate. Remember that it would cause your lender time and trouble to evict you. They will usually prefer to let you keep the loan going if you can show that you can manage.

If you are under pressure from your lenders because you have arrears, see Chapter six for how you can try to clear them. However, if you want to show your lender that your arrears can be cleared, you must at the same time convince them (and yourself) that you will be able to keep up your payments in the future. This chapter will show you how to do this. Even if you cannot come to any agreement and you are taken to court to be evicted, do not give up hope. Tell the court what you have suggested. The court may agree that your proposals are reasonable and give you time to show that you can manage.

If, when you took out your mortgage, you also took out an insurance policy (sometimes called a **'mortgage instalment protection plan'**) to cover your mortgage payments in the event of sickness or unemployment and one of these reasons is the cause of your difficulties, then make sure you claim on the policy straightaway. There can be short time limits for making claims. (See pages 4 and 9 for more information on mortgage protection plans.)

GETTING HELP AND ADVICE

Much will depend on how you set out your suggestions for paying in the future. If your lender does not agree to your proposals, or you need help to draw up the proposals, seek advice from one of the agencies listed in Appendix 7.

This guide is designed to help you understand your mortgage and work out a strategy for solving problems that you have with it. But it is not an admission of failure to seek help or advice from other agencies. Indeed, there are a number of reasons why you may not be able to make the best use of the information contained in this book without such help. For example:

- ☐ It is useful to have an impartial 'third party' to look at your situation and help you get your problems in perspective. Advisers find that people with mortgage problems can either exaggerate or underestimate the seriousness of their situation and respond inappropriately as a result.

- ☐ Many of the problems people with mortgage arrears encounter are so complex that they cannot be fully covered in a book like this and you will need more expert advice. We have tried to indicate where this is most likely to be the case.

- ☐ While the recent growth in mortgage arrears has led many lenders to be more sympathetic to, and understanding of, borrowers' problems, advisers still find situations where, as a result of a lack of understanding or organisational problems, perfectly reasonable proposals from borrowers are rejected. Very often the intervention of an advice agency with a proven track record will persuade the lender to reconsider.

You can get help from a variety of sources. You should probably contact a specialist housing aid centre or money advice service. Most large local authorities and a number of smaller ones will provide these services. Housing aid centres are run by local authority housing departments. Money advisers might be based in the housing department, the consumer protection department or the welfare rights service.

Independent money advice services are run by Citizens Advice Bureaux in many areas, and independent housing advice is provided by SHAC in London and Shelter in other parts of the country (see Appendix 7 for addresses).

If you cannot locate any of these services contact a generalist advice agency, either through the National Association of Citizens' Advice Bureaux or through the Federation of Independent Advice Centres – or you may find one in Thompson's Directory (see Appendix 7). If they are unable to help you themselves they should be able to refer you on elsewhere.

Some solicitors have considerable expertise in advising people with mortgage problems, and if you qualify for legal aid under the Green Form scheme (or its Scottish equivalent, Advice and Assistance on a pink form) you could contact one of them (see Appendix 6). But make sure that they genuinely have this knowledge; there are many areas of law and no one solicitor can possibly be expert in all of them.

IF YOU HAVE ONE MORTGAGE

Making reduced payments for a temporary period

If you are experiencing a temporary reduction in income – for example, because of a temporary illness or industrial dispute – your lender may be prepared to accept lower payments and defer part of your interest payments for a period.

Because interest is deferred, you will have to pay it back when your income increases, so your lender will probably only agree to reduced payments if your situation is likely to improve in the foreseeable future.

It is also in your own interests to make this arrangement over the shortest period possible because the amount of money you owe your lender is going to increase and this can very easily spiral out of control. If your lender does agree to this, make sure that it is put in writing, along with the terms for repayment of the arrears which arise as a result and any other conditions. Do not agree to any terms which you are not certain you can meet.

Making reduced payments for a longer period

Capital repayment mortgage

There are two ways in which your repayment arrangement can be changed to cut your costs if you have a capital repayment mortgage:

- [ ] by paying mortgage interest only;
- [ ] by extending the term of the mortgage.

Pay mortgage interest only

Your lender may agree to accept payments of interest alone and allow you to put off paying back the capital you owe while your present difficulties last. The amount of difference this will make to your monthly payments will depend on the length of time you have had your mortgage. As shown in the diagram on page 3, the repayment of capital forms only a small part of your monthly payments in the first few years but the amount grows later on. This rearrangement need only be temporary and should not involve much work for your lender. It is worth asking them to agree to help you in this way even if it makes only a small difference to your monthly costs. You should certainly do so if you are receiving income support, as your benefit will only cover the interest part of your mortgage payments. If you are receiving income support and getting help with the mortgage interest from the Benefits Agency, in most cases, this is now paid directly to the lender (see page 37). This may help persuade the lender to accept interest only for a period.

Ask to pay mortgage interest only whether your drop in income is temporary or permanent as it is the only way to get an immediate reduction in your costs.

Extend the term of the mortgage.

You can ask your lender to extend the mortgage term. In practice, this means asking them to make a new mortgage arrangement which will give you more time to repay the money you still owe. This will reduce the capital part of your monthly payments. The amount of interest you have to pay each month will, however, remain the same.

Because this arrangement is only going to affect the capital part of your repayments, there is no point in suggesting this to your lender if they will agree to accept interest only. If your lender will accept interest only now, you could ask for an extension of the term when you can afford to start repaying the capital again, if you still need to budget carefully. If your lender has refused to accept interest only payments you should ask to extend the term whether your drop in income is temporary or permanent.

How to negotiate with your lender

Write to your lender stating:

- ☐ your name, address and mortgage account number;
- ☐ your present financial difficulties, why they have arisen and how long they are going to last;

- ☐ that you wish either to pay interest only or to extend the mortgage term;
- ☐ what your income is going to be in future and how you are going to keep up the new payments.

Remember to keep a copy of your letter.

> **Special note for separated partners:** You should check pages 115-116 to see other information you should include in your letter.

Endowment mortgage

There are two ways in which your repayment arrangements can be changed to cut your costs if you have an endowment mortgage:

- ☐ by changing to a capital repayment mortgage;
- ☐ by paying interest only (see page 67).

Change to a capital repayment mortgage

This means that you stop paying the endowment policy premiums and instead start repaying capital. Interest payments on the money you owe will, of course, continue. Depending on the type of endowment mortgage you have, the cost of paying interest plus repayment of capital may be less than the cost of paying interest plus your policy premium.

It is possible to obtain a temporary suspension of policy premiums if you have an endowment mortgage. However, if difficulties are likely to last, it may be better to change to a capital repayment mortgage even if the difference in the cost is small because it is easier to rearrange the costs of a capital repayment mortgage.

If you do decide to change from an endowment mortgage to a capital repayment mortgage, you will first need to get information from your insurance company.

Write to the insurance company stating:

- ☐ your name, address and insurance policy number (if you know it);
- ☐ that you want to know the **surrender value** of your policy. (This is the amount the company will pay you in cash if you stop paying the premiums and cancel the policy);
- ☐ that you want to know the **paid-up value** of your policy. (This is the amount of money which the company will still agree to pay out at the

end of the term or on your death if you stop paying premiums but do not cancel the policy);

- [ ] that you need this information because you are hoping to change the terms of your mortgage.

Remember to keep a copy of your letter.

You should avoid surrendering your life policy if possible, particularly if the policy has been going for many years, as the surrender value will be much less than the policy is worth. If you are not able to keep up the payments on the policy, you are likely to get more if you sell the policy to an investor rather than surrendering it to the insurance company. You should speak to an insurance broker about this.

If you do surrender your life policy, it is best to try to do this on its anniversary. If the policy is surrendered in the middle of the year, profits for that year will be lost.

> **Special note for separated partners:** If you are not named on the life policy you may not be able to get any surrender or paid-up value unless your partner cooperates. However, this will not necessarily prevent your lender from changing the endowment mortgage to a capital repayment mortgage and you should certainly ask them to do this if it would help.

Once you have received the above information from the insurance company, you will need to negotiate with your lender. Your insurance policy is your lender's guarantee that their capital will be repaid and it is part of your mortgage agreement that you will pay the premiums, so you will have to discuss with them the terms on which you can make the change to a capital repayment mortgage.

If your mortgage is directly with an insurance company, or your building society is not willing to change the terms of the mortgage you may be able to get a new mortgage for the whole amount and pay off your existing lender (see page 68). *Write* to your lender stating:

- [ ] your name, address and mortgage account number;
- [ ] your present financial difficulties, why they have arisen, and how long they are likely to last;
- [ ] the insurance company's figures for the surrender value and the paid-up value of your policy;
- [ ] that you wish to cancel your policy and to use the surrender value towards

the mortgage arrears, or to keep the surrender value to use for some necessary expense – for example, house maintenance or paying another bill. Ask for the surrender value if you need the cash now; *or*

- [ ] that you wish to stop paying your policy premiums but *not* to cancel your policy. You would like that part of your mortgage which would be covered by the paid-up value to continue on the endowment basis, and only the remainder to be transferred to the capital repayment basis. If you do not need cash now, this might be a better choice as your outgoings would be lower. This is because you will be paying interest only and will not have to make capital repayments on that part of the mortgage which will be covered by the paid-up value;

- [ ] what your income is going to be in future and how you are going to keep up the new payments;

- [ ] that you wish to know what legal expenses, if any, you will be charged when the mortgage is changed.

Make sure you keep a copy of your letter.

Remember: if you do convert to a capital repayment mortgage, then you should probably take out a mortgage protection policy to cover the risk of your dying before the end of the term (see page 4).

Pay interest only

A change to a capital repayment mortgage will take some time to come into effect. In the meantime, your lender may agree to let you stop paying your policy premiums which will mean an immediate cut in your costs. If you are receiving income support this will be an important change, because your benefit will only cover the interest payments.

However, many insurance policies are automatically cancelled if a certain number of premiums are not paid – for example, for six months or more – so your lender may only agree to this kind of arrangement in the *very* short term.

IF YOU HAVE TWO OR MORE MORTGAGES

If you have more than one mortgage, you will need to arrange your borrowing on the cheapest possible basis. The cost of your first mortgage may be able to be reduced in one of the ways already described above.

However, your second and later mortgages may be more expensive than your first mortgage, because you are likely to be paying a higher interest rate over a shorter term. If you have a high cost second loan you should consider taking out a loan at a cheaper interest rate to pay it back and cut your costs. This is known as refinancing the loan.

Remember: If you are seeking to refinance a second loan, do not ask for the first and second loans to be added together to form a new single mortgage, as this will take the whole loan out of MIRAS resulting in a higher monthly payment. Tax relief will then have to be claimed direct from the Inland Revenue. The second loan can be refinanced as a separate loan.

Making a fresh start

You should consider refinancing if:

- ☐ **you have more than one mortgage,** and your second and later mortgages are more expensive than your first mortgage;
- ☐ **you want to rearrange** an endowment mortgage and your present lender cannot or will not do this;
- ☐ **you had a mortgage from your last employer** who offered you a cut-price interest rate, but you have now lost your job or want to change jobs;
- ☐ **you had a bridging loan from your bank** to help you buy your home and you now have to repay it.

Who can you ask for a refinanced mortgage?

If you are refinancing a second loan, try asking your first lender if they will consider this; otherwise you should ask a building society because they usually lend at the cheapest rate. If one of your present loans was used for a non-housing purpose, they may be reluctant to help you, but very often will have the power to help. Building societies have wide powers to lend money against the security of property. Although societies lend money to buy, improve or repair property, they can make secured or unsecured loans for other reasons.

Ask your local authority for a new mortgage if your first mortgage is with that local authority. If your local authority cannot help you with a new mortgage themselves, they may be able to help by referring you to a local building society. Local authorities have powers to guarantee mortgages. If you can persuade your local authority to offer such a guarantee this may help persuade a building society to give you a mortgage. You should contact the local housing department and, if you have children, the social services department.

Do not ask a finance company to give you a new mortgage, because their expensive loan could land you in even more trouble.

How much are you likely to get?

If you are working: Different lenders have different ways of calculating how much they will lend. Generally, lenders will multiply your gross annual income by a certain figure, and this figure may change when interest rates change.

Example

Jim Smith earns £16,000 a year and his wife earns £7,000. Their lender's policy is to multiply his gross income by two and a half times and to add on one times her gross income. They could hope to get a new mortgage for £47,000. That is:

(£16,000 x 2.5 = £40,000) plus (£7,000 x 1 = £7,000).

You may be able to get more than this if you need it. You will have to show exactly how you will meet the new payments out of your present income.

Check the amount of your new payments using Appendix 1. You should also bear in mind that there will be survey, legal and other fees connected with arranging a new mortgage, so unless the savings that you are going to make are greater than these new costs it is not worth changing your loan.

If you are receiving income support: You will have to show the lender that your local Benefits Agency office will meet all or part of the interest payments on the amount you need for the new mortgage. For more information on this, see page 36.

How to negotiate with your lenders

There are two steps to take. First, you must find out how much you owe on your second and later mortgages, including any arrears.

Second, you must ask your first lender to consider granting you a second mortgage for the amount you need to refinance your other loans.

Write to all your lenders, other than the first, stating:

- ☐ your name, address and mortgage account number;
- ☐ that you want to pay back (or redeem) your loans;
- ☐ that you want a **redemption figure**. (This is the amount you still owe your lender. It will include the capital you have not yet paid back and

any arrears.) The figure may be higher than you expect, both because some companies charge interest on arrears and because some charge a fee for allowing you to redeem before the end of the term. If you think that the fee is unreasonably high, do not accept it. Get advice from one of the agencies listed in Appendix 7.

Remember to keep a copy of this letter.

Next, *write* to the lender from whom you want a new mortgage stating:

- ☐ your name, address and mortgage account number (if you already have an account with that lender);

- ☐ the amount of mortgage you will need. Give the redemption figures that you have received from other lenders, stating the month to which they apply;

- ☐ your present total income. This should include your gross income (before any deductions), that of any members of your family living with you, and all the benefits you get, such as child benefit, family credit, income support, housing benefit and national insurance benefits;

- ☐ that you have calculated you will be able to manage the new mortgage payments (see Appendix 1) as well as your other commitments. Show that you have considered costs such as travelling to work and child-minding where appropriate.

Remember to keep a copy of this letter.

You must check the redemption figures with the lenders when you know the date on which the new mortgage will be granted. This is because the figures may change from month to month, depending on how many more payments you make and on whether the rate of interest changes. If the redemption figures do go up, you will have to ask your new lender to cover this increase.

CONSUMER CREDIT ACT LOANS

If you have a loan which is regulated by the Consumer Credit Act 1974 you may be able to get the repayments reduced by way of a **time order** from the county court (see page 83). Generally, loans to individuals, where the amount borrowed is less than £15,000, are governed by the 1974 Act.

Although you may have to apply to the court for a time order, it may be possible to negotiate with the lender without having to go to court. For details of how to apply for a time order, see page 84.

APPEALS TO LENDERS

All building societies now have an internal complaints procedure. If you are dissatisfied with any decision that your building society has made about your loan, you can ask for the decision to be reconsidered through this procedure.

If you are still dissatisfied after the outcome of the internal complaints procedure, you can refer your case to the Building Societies Ombudsman. You should contact the Ombudsman's office (see Appendix 7 for address) if you believe your building society has treated you unfairly or has been guilty of maladministration (including inefficiency or undue delay) in a way that results in you losing money or suffering inconvenience. If the Ombudsman's office can deal with your complaint, they may try to negotiate a settlement with the lender. If that fails, they will make their own impartial decision as to who is right.

Outside of the formal complaints procedures, it is often helpful, if you feel that you have been unfairly treated, to write direct to the Chair or Chief Executive of your building society asking her/him to investigate the matter.

Anyone applying to the local authority for a mortgage can ask their local councillor for help in changing an unfavourable decision. Your local town hall or library can give you the names of your local councillors.

If you feel the local authority has treated you unfairly or discriminated against you, you can make a complaint to the Local Government Ombudsman (see Appendix 7). The Ombudsman has considerable powers to investigate your complaint and can recommend that the local authority puts right any wrong decisions and compensates you. However, this is not an appeals procedure and if the Ombudsman feels that your complaint does not involve 'maladministration', s/he does not have to investigate it at all. Because the Ombudsman will investigate the complaint very thoroughly it may take several months before you receive a decision.

If you have borrowed money from any other source and are having difficulties making the repayments, write to the lender's head office to ask them to reconsider any unfavourable decisions made.

CHAPTER SIX

Dealing with arrears

If you do not make your monthly payments, your lender can apply to the court for an order giving them the right to evict you from your home, so that it can be sold and the proceeds used to pay off the loan.

However, it is never too late for you to take steps to try to keep your home. Even if your position seems hopeless, there are several ways in which you can arrange to clear your arrears. If you can do this and, at the same time, cut your future mortgage costs (see Chapter five) and increase your income (see Chapter two, Chapter three and Chapter four), you will be able to keep your home knowing that you can manage from now on.

This chapter explains the steps your lenders will take to get their money back when you fall behind with your payments. It goes on to explain what you must do to stop the action they are taking and to bring your mortgage(s) back up to date. If you would like advice, contact one of the organisations listed in Appendix 7.

There are special rules which apply to loans regulated by the Consumer Credit Act 1974, and in England and Wales the court has specific powers to help reduce the rate of payment. These are dealt with on pages 83-84.

HOW LENDERS RECLAIM A LOAN

In England and Wales, any lender who has a 'charge' on your home will be able to apply to the county court for a possession order. In Scotland the application is made to the Sheriff Court for an ejection order. To find out whether a lender has a charge on your property see page 2. Once the order has been made, the lender can take over your home and sell it to get back their money. The stages of your lender's action are as follows:

- ☐ As soon as your mortgage payments stop, *your lender will write* and ask you to make arrangements to bring your payments up to date.

- ☐ If you continue to miss making your mortgage repayments and/or fail to clear your arrears, your lender will write again, *threatening legal proceedings*.

This means that they are thinking of instructing their solicitors to apply to the court for an order for possession of your home.

In Scotland, a creditor may either serve a 'Calling Up Notice' requiring discharge of the debt or, serve a 'Notice of Default'. If the debtor fails to comply with these, or, in the case of the second, does not successfully object in the Sheriff Court, the creditor is entitled to seek to repossess and sell the property. The court cannot reduce repayments to help the debtor.

In cases governed by the Consumer Credit Act 1974, the lender will send you a 'default notice' telling you to pay the arrears and threatening to take you to court if you do not. At this point you can apply for a **time order** to reduce the payments (see page 84).

☐ *Your lender will pass details of your mortgage to their solicitors.* From this time on the solicitors will act on the lender's behalf, but you can still negotiate with the lender direct.

☐ *The court will send you a summons.* This is a form which tells you that you are being taken to court and gives the date of the hearing. The summons includes a document headed 'Particulars of Claim' which your lender's solicitor will have drafted, setting out the details of the mortgage agreement and the amount of arrears alleged. Attached is another form which you should fill in and return within 14 days, stating whether or not you agree with the facts your lenders have given and what you are proposing to do about them. In Scotland, the document is called an 'Initial Writ' and will include a 'Condescendence' which will give the equivalent details. The debtor has 21 days to return a Notice of Intention to Defend.

☐ *The court hearing will take place.* You will have the chance to state your circumstances and explain the arrangements you are able to make to clear the arrears and keep up the full monthly payments in the future. If you are in a position to pay off all the arrears there and then, and provide evidence that you will be able to make the full payments in future, the court will probably refuse to make any kind of possession order against you. However, even if you cannot pay off all the arrears straightaway, the court has wide powers to adjourn the proceedings or make a suspended possession order. A suspended possession order will not entitle your lender to evict you so long as you keep up the payments ordered by the court. You should explain your proposals for clearing the arrears to the court (see page 77).

If you do not keep up the payments your lender will be able to apply for a *possession warrant* and have you evicted by the court bailiffs without having to arrange another hearing in court. When a suspended possession order is made you can ask the court to order that a possession warrant should not be issued without a further hearing for the court to give permission. It will be at the court's discretion to agree to this part of the suspended order.

None of the above applies in Scotland, where lenders obtain court orders which they will sometimes voluntarily hold in suspension if agreed repayments are adhered to.

If the court decides your position is a hopeless one, it will make an *outright possession order*, ordering possession within, normally, 28 days.

- *The lender can apply for a possession warrant on or after the date specified in the court order*; you do not have to leave on that date. Once the court office has processed the application, it will give the necessary details to the bailiffs, who will fix a date and time for the eviction. The bailiffs will then write to you giving you the eviction date. You are normally given a week or two's notice of the date for the eviction by the bailiff. In Scotland, Sheriff's Officers are the equivalent of bailiffs and will operate in a similar way.
- *If you are still there when the bailiffs arrive*, they will evict you from your home and either remove your belongings at the same time or make arrangements with you for their removal.

HOW TO KEEP YOUR HOME

It is very important that you do not stop paying your mortgage completely, just because you cannot afford the whole amount. You should pay what you can while you take steps to lower your mortgage costs and increase your income (see Chapters two, three, four and five). To work out what you can afford, draw up a financial statement (see page 75). You also need to make sure that you will be able to manage in the future. You must take steps to stop your lender's action and see about clearing your arrears. You can use your financial statement to show your lender what you can afford. The Council of Mortgage Lenders and the government issued a joint statement in December 1991. This said 'Where borrowers have suffered a significant reduction in their income, but are making a reasonable regular payment, lenders do not seek to take possession.' This has now been incorporated into the *Council of Mortgage Lenders Arrears Management Manual*, Section D, paragraph 14 (a). Interest which is not paid is added to the loan and will have to be repaid at some time in the future.

Drawing up a financial statement

A financial statement will be essential in helping you to negotiate with your lender (and any other creditors) to reach realistic repayment arrangements. It will also ensure that you do not overcommit yourself on offers to clear arrears. You can use your financial statement in court, as evidence to show you have carefully worked out your financial situation and are making reasonable proposals.

The financial statement should set out clear details of your income and expenditure on a weekly or monthly basis (see Appendix 8 for an example of a financial statement). When calculating expenditure it is important not to underestimate what you spend and to allow for even very small items such as birthdays or Christmas presents. It is common to underestimate how much you spend on food and household items and not to allow for unforeseen expenses. When working out how much you spend, it is wise to add in a 10 per cent cushion for unforeseen expenses. Your financial statement must be as accurate as possible because it is the basis on which you will make offers of repayment. It is important to keep to any offers you make in order to prevent action which could lead to the loss of your home.

Stopping your lender's action

You must act quickly, especially if the court or the bailiff (in Scotland, Sheriff Officer) is already involved. It is never too late to try to keep your home. What you should do depends on how far your lender's action has gone.

☐ *You are under pressure from your lender but they have not yet applied to the court for a hearing* (see page 72). Write back to your lender straightaway. Tell them that you are making every effort to clear your arrears, and that you will let them know your proposals on this within, say, one month. Explain how your circumstances have changed and how you hope to meet your mortgage payments in future. Ask them to help you cut your mortgage costs in any of the ways appropriate (see Chapter five). If you are unable to meet the full monthly payment, ask them to accept a lower regular amount. Use your financial statement to help you negotiate. If your lender refuses to negotiate with you and says that the action is going ahead, ask for help from a person in higher authority and send them a copy of your earlier letter. The person to write to is the general manager of your building society or finance company, or your local councillor if your loan is from the local authority.

In cases where the agreement is regulated by the Consumer Credit Act, you may be able to stop proceedings by reducing the repayments to a rate you can manage by way of a 'time order' from the county court (or Sheriff Court – see page 83).

- ☐ *You have received a court summons* (in Scotland, an *Initial Writ*) (see page 73). If you have not already been writing to your lender as above, you should try to get the court hearing adjourned to give you time to look at ways of clearing your arrears.

  Ideally, you want to get your lender's agreement to the adjournment. If there is time before the court hearing, write to your lender's solicitor setting out how you intend to clear the arrears (see page 77) and make future payments. Ask the solicitor to agree to adjourn the hearing to give you the time you need to rearrange your finances as suggested in Chapters two, three and four. If your lender's solicitors refuse to agree to an adjournment and you believe they are being unreasonable in not agreeing to one, it is worth considering making an application to the court for an adjournment. In Scotland, it may be easier to ask for the case to be 'sisted' (ie, put to sleep) pending negotiations and a repayment programme.

  In England and Wales your lender's solicitor should be given at least two days' notice of the application, but give shorter notice if you have to.

  You should complete the reply to the summons and return it to court. This has four pages of questions about your mortgage and your circumstances. It is important that you address the following points:

  – Check that the lender's claim is correct. Do not assume their figure for arrears is right – check it against your statements and other records.

  – Check that all the arrears claimed are payments due under the mortgage agreement as possession can be only be granted on the basis of these sums. If a large part of the sum claimed is interest on arrears, legal or administrative charges, it may be possible to clear the genuine arrears and avoid a possession order.

  – The form asks you about your financial circumstances, so make sure that you include all the information contained in your financial statement.

  – You should explain how you got in arrears, and briefly mention any actions by your lender which have made your situation worse. However, the court is going to be most interested in how you can make adequate payments in future and this must be explained clearly.

- ☐ *The court hearing is to take place* (see page 73). It is essential that you attend court. A recent study has shown that two-thirds of borrowers who attend court have their possession orders suspended, while only two-fifths of borrowers who do not attend achieve this. If, for some reason, you have not been able to prepare your case and negotiate with your lender before the hearing (perhaps you learned about it too late), you can ask the judge (in England and Wales, the district judge, in Scotland, the Sheriff) to agree to an adjournment. In any event, you must go along to the court on the date of the hearing and be ready to put your case, because the adjournment may not be allowed. It is a good idea to take a friend or adviser with you (see Appendix 7 and page 62). In Scotland, only you or your solicitor can address the court. Remember that the case is all about money. If you are arguing against an outright possession order being granted, you will have to explain how you are going to clear the arrears (see below) and pay your mortgage in future. The judge will be more interested in this than in the reasons for your difficulties.

How to prepare your case

Before you read this section, you should consider getting legal help (see Appendix 6 which gives the background to the Legal Aid Scheme), or advice and representation from one of the organisations listed in Appendix 7. Your basic task is to show how you can clear your arrears either with a lump-sum payment or gradually, over a period of months, or by a combination of the two. Tell the court:

- how much money, if any, you have, or will have, to pay as a lump sum;
- the steps you are taking to raise a lump sum;
- how much you are certain of being able to pay each month to clear the arrears. Use your financial statement to help you show this;
- the steps you are hoping to take to lower your mortgage costs and/or increase your income so that you can manage in future.

How much should you offer to pay?

Do not overcommit yourself. You must balance the need to clear your debt as soon as possible with the importance of making an offer which you know you will be able to keep up. Use your financial statement to show how much you can offer. Do not be put off from making an offer in court because your lender has already told you that it is too low or that the arrears must be cleared more quickly. If you are on income support explain whether direct payments are being made to meet the interest and something towards the arrears (see page 79). It is up to the judge to decide what is reasonable.

If you make an offer in court which you are unable to keep, it will be harder (if not impossible) to convince the judge of your good faith when you return to fight a possession application for the second time. On the other hand, the more quickly you can offer to repay the arrears, the better your chances are of staying in your home. Most courts will suspend the possession order if you can show that you can clear the arrears within two years while, at the same time, paying the normal monthly instalments as they fall due. If the judge does not accept your case against the possession order, you should ask for enough time to sell your home and find alternative accommodation (see Chapter eight). In Scotland, all you can do is convince the Sheriff to continue the case and trust that you can convince the lender to accept repayments. If your lender has been granted a possession order and has already applied for a possession warrant (see page 74), you can apply to the court for another hearing if you have any new proposals which you were not able to make at the last hearing. You can do this whatever stage your lender's action has reached as long as you have not actually been evicted. The court has power to prevent an eviction even where a possession warrant has been obtained and a date for the eviction set, but you will have to move very fast to get a hearing in time.

At the same time, write to your lender's solicitors setting out your new proposals and enclosing your financial statement. It is vital that you apply for a fresh hearing if you were not able to put your case at the last one. This may have been because you were sick or at work, or did not know about the legal action, for instance, if you are separated and the information was sent to your partner only.

Note: This provision does not apply in Scotland.

'Third party' loans

If you have agreed to let another person secure a loan on your house, and the risk has not been properly explained to you, it may be possible to argue that the charge is not valid because the lender was in breach of their legal responsibility to ensure that your interests were protected. This would apply to a loan taken out by your partner or ex-partner, or a relative or friend. It might even apply to a joint loan taken out in your name if you did not benefit from it, for instance if your partner used it for their own business or other expenditure. You will have to convince the court that the third party used 'undue influence' to persuade you to agree to this. If you think that this is the case, you should urgently seek expert advice from a solicitor or money adviser.

CLEARING YOUR MORTGAGE ARREARS

You can clear your arrears by paying a lump sum to your lender or by paying off a little each month over a specific period of time, or by a combination of both. Your first move must be to find out exactly how much you owe your lender(s) now. Write to each of them and ask for a statement of your account(s).

> **Special note for separated partners:** if the mortgage is not in your name, you may find that the lender is unwilling to give you the figures you need. There are other options you can follow:
> - try to get your partner to give your lender written permission to release the figures to you;
> - explain to your lender that you wish to make the repayments in future and to clear the arrears. If you are married, stress that you have the right to make payments in your spouse's place under Section 1(5) of the Matrimonial Homes Act 1983 (in Scotland, the Matrimonial Homes (Family Protection) (Scotland) Act 1981). State that you need to know details of the accounts so that you can make the payments.

Direct payments

Since 1992 most income support claimants have had their mortgage interest paid direct to their lenders after they have been on income support for 16 weeks. The *Council of Mortgage Lenders Arrears Management Manual*, Section D, para 14(c) states that 'In the knowledge that Income Support will in future be paid direct, lenders will not take possession in cases where mortgage interest payments are covered by income support.'

The Benefits Agency can also pay direct to your lender an amount towards mortgage arrears. They will do this if they think it is in your family's best interests. This gives the lender the reassurance that the arrears are being reduced. At 1994/95 rates, the Benefits Agency can deduct up to £2.30 per mortgage debt. They can deduct a maximum of £6.90 a week from your income support if you are in arrears with three debts.

How to raise a lump sum

There are at least five different ways of trying to do this.

Apply to your local Benefits Agency office

- *If you are already receiving income support*, make sure that you are getting the right amount (see Appendix 3). If you have not told the Benefits

Agency about an increase in the mortgage interest rate you have been charged, you could have been underpaid by the Benefits Agency. If, for any reason, you have not been receiving your full entitlement, write to the local office and ask them to review the amount of benefit they have been paying and to pay any arrears due, back to the date when you claimed benefit. Arrears of income support can be backdated by up to 12 months or even longer, if the Benefits Agency has made a mistake. For more information on backdating income support see page 47.

- ☐ *If you are not claiming income support*, check whether you qualify for it (see Chapter three). The local office has the power to backdate your claim for up to 12 months if there is a good reason why your claim was late. For instance, you may have claimed another benefit, such as unemployment benefit, thinking this would cover your needs and now find that you were entitled to some income support as well. You may have been wrongly advised by the Benefits Agency, an advice centre or a solicitor that you were not entitled to claim; or there may be other good reasons why you did not claim earlier. Ask the adjudication officer to use her/his power to backdate, and appeal if you are refused (see page 47).

- ☐ *If you are not entitled to income support*, check whether you can claim family credit (see page 14). Family credit can also be backdated for up to 12 months if you can show good cause for a late claim.

> **Special note for separated partners:** you may get a backpayment if you have not claimed income support for your housing costs, in the belief that your partner was paying the mortgage interest. This would be good cause for not claiming.

If you have children under 16, apply to your local social services department. Write, asking them to consider making you a payment using their power under Section 17 of the Children Act 1989 (in Scotland, the equivalent is s12 of the Social Work (Scotland) Act) and explain that you and your children are threatened with eviction and homelessness because of your mortgage arrears. Most social services departments do not have much money available and will usually want to know that you have already applied to your social security office if you are now receiving income support.

Change your type of mortgage

If you have an endowment mortgage, ask your lender to convert it to a capital repayment one and to allow you to use the 'surrender value' of your life policy to repay your mortgage arrears (see page 65). The surrender values of endowment policies are ignored as capital and income for income support purposes.

Ask your lender to 'capitalise' your mortgage arrears. This means that your lender will add the amount of your arrears to the capital you still owe and arrange for you to repay this higher amount as a new mortgage. Your lender might be more willing to consider this if you can show that you have already tried other ways of raising a lump sum. You might find it easier to persuade the lender to 'capitalise' the arrears if your local authority agrees to guarantee the lender against financial loss in the event of your not paying the mortgage in future. If you have children, you should definitely ask the housing department, and also the social services department, to help with a guarantee (see pages 80 and 135).

If arrears of mortgage interest are capitalised and they exceed 12 months' arrears or £1,000, whichever is the greater, and no arrangements to reduce the arrears have been made, the lender has to inform the Inland Revenue who may take your loan out of the MIRAS system (see page 12). Tax relief on interest would then have to be claimed direct from the Inland Revenue.

However, if satisfactory arrangements have been made to reduce arrears even where capitalised interest exceeds 12 months' arrears or £1,000, the lender does not have to notify the Inland Revenue. For loans taken out before 1 August 1988, the limit of 12 months' arrears or £1,000 extends to each borrower if the loan is in joint names, unless the joint borrowers are married. For all loans taken out after 1 August 1988, the single limit will apply.

If you are on income support you should be getting some help towards mortgage interest payments. However, if you had arrears prior to your claim for benefit or if arrears have built up while you have been on benefit, the Benefits Agency will generally not help with interest payments now due in respect of those arrears. If you capitalise these arrears, interest on the capitalised arrears will generally not be met by the Benefits Agency.

Income support will, however, pay interest on arrears if:

☐ the arrears arose because the Benefits Agency only paid 50 per cent of your interest during the first 16 weeks of your claim (see page 40);

☐ you have a 'low-start' mortgage which defers interest payments for at least two years, and arrears accumulate as a result.

In addition, it is possible that you could have claimed income support before you did. If you can persuade the Benefits Agency to accept a backdated claim (see page 47), you should get the mortgage interest that was due at that time and possibly interest on the arrears as well. If you think that this may be the case, you should get further advice (see Appendix 7).

Apply to a charity

The *Directory of Grant Making Trusts*, which you can find at your local library, has a full list of charities and gives a brief outline of the categories of people they are prepared to consider for grants. It is always worth looking through this book under such headings as the occupations of your family, particular illnesses which may have affected you and your family, and the areas you have lived in or in which you were born.

Find one or two charities which might consider helping you. Write and ask for a grant to cover your mortgage arrears. Explain that you and your family are threatened with eviction and homelessness, that you will be able to make your full mortgage payments in future, and that this single payment will enable you to keep your home.

Important: never take out another mortgage in order to pay off arrears on your present one. If you cannot pay one mortgage, how will you pay two?

Increase your monthly payments

Using your financial statement, work out carefully how much extra you could afford to pay your lender each month over and above your mortgage repayments. Check Chapters two, three and four to make sure that your income is as high as possible. Check Chapter five to make sure that your mortgage costs are as low as possible. Encourage your lender to agree to any rearrangements you can suggest, by pointing out that the reduction in your mortgage costs will give you spare cash each month to put towards your mortgage arrears. Some lenders may agree to accept interest only and suspend the capital part of your repayments while you are trying to clear arrears. You can pay what would have been the capital part of the payment (and a bit extra if you can afford it) towards clearing the arrears.

Negotiate with your lender(s)

If you have more than one mortgage in arrears and cannot raise enough to cover them all, do not repay one in full and leave yourself unable to offer any money to the other(s). Try and spread what you have raised among them.

When you share it out, you may have to give more to the lender to whom you owe the most or who is the most advanced in their legal proceedings against you.

If you cannot make a lump-sum payment to clear all your arrears, you will have to pay off the remaining amount in monthly instalments. Work out how much you can afford each month and how many months it would take you to clear the arrears if you repaid at this rate. Your lender will be pressing you to clear the arrears in as short a time as possible. They may suggest a time limit which would mean higher instalments than you could afford. Do not agree to this. Write to your lender enclosing your financial statement and state what you can pay each month and start paying this immediately. The statement should list your income and outgoings, in detail, on a monthly basis. Your lender may not be satisfied, but remember that if they take you to court your regular payments will help convince the judge that you made your offer in good faith.

It may also be helpful in persuading the lender to give you time to pay off the arrears, if you can produce an estate agent's valuation of your home to show that there is substantial equity (see page 2) and that as a result the lender is not at risk. Such a valuation can also be used in court. However, a valuation which shows that there is no or very little equity will be damaging and should not be used in your negotiations.

CONSUMER CREDIT ACT LOANS

The local county court (in Scotland, the Sheriff Court) is given wide powers under the Consumer Credit Act 1974 to assist borrowers who have difficulties in paying loans which are governed by the 1974 Act. Broadly, loans of £15,000 or less made to one or more individuals will be regulated by the Act unless they are 'exempt agreements'. The main types of exempt agreements are agreements with local authorities, building societies and similar bodies for house purchase, repairs and improvements. Although the details of exempt agreement provisions are complicated, it should be clear from the written agreement itself whether the 1974 Act applies. If you are in any doubt you should ask the lender for a copy of the written agreement.

The main type of help available is a **time order** which you can ask the court to make under section 129 of the Consumer Credit Act 1974. This allows the court to order that you pay 'any sum owed' to the lender, at such rate as the court considers reasonable, taking into account your financial position. This means that you can ask the court to give you time to pay the arrears at a rate that you can afford; a financial statement will be essential so you can show the court how much this is. Section 129 would also seem to allow the court to set the rate for repayment of all money owed by you to the lender, and not just the arrears, in those cases where the loan agreement provides that all outstanding capital and interest becomes immediately payable on demand or on default of a payment by the borrower. Most loan agreements provide for this type of early repayment when a borrower starts getting into arrears.

You might be able to persuade the lender to allow you to repay the loan by reduced instalments under threat of you applying to the court for a time order if the lender does not agree. The earliest point at which you can apply for a time order is when you receive the 'default notice' which lenders are obliged to send you before taking any steps to recover money owed or to repossess the property. If you wish to apply for a time order at this stage you need to fill in a form N440 available from your local county court. There is no equivalent form in Scotland. The Sheriff Court Rules are being examined at present. This form requires you to set out your financial position. It is quite easy to complete. There is a fee of £40 to pay, but you may be able to persuade the court to waive this fee if you write to the court beforehand setting out your financial position and saying that you would like them to waive the court fee.

Alternatively you can apply for a time order as part of the court proceedings brought against you by the lender. You will need to fill in the defence form which comes with the summons asking that the court makes a time order and send it back to the court. You should put your financial details on the defence form. There is no fee to pay if you apply for a time order as part of the possession proceedings. However, it is better to apply for the time order before the lender starts possession proceedings as the benefits of any reduction in the rate of repayment will only take effect from the date of the hearing of the case.

The parts of the Consumer Credit Act which allow courts to make time orders are still a matter of controversy and the full extent of the courts' powers needs to be clarified. Three cases are due to be heard in the Court of Appeal in March 1995 which should result in a definitive judgment, but this decision may in turn be the subject of a further appeal to the House of Lords. Given this uncertainty, you should consider getting advice at the earliest opportunity (see Appendix 7 for a list of advice agencies).

It is also possible to ask the court to change the terms of the agreement separate from the time order provisions. This can be done under the 'extortionate credit bargain' provisions of the 1974 Act. The court can do this if the interest rate charged is exorbitant or the loan agreement otherwise contravenes ordinary principles of fair trading. Although the courts have not used these powers very regularly to re-open loan agreements, it may be possible to get the agreement changed by the court if the interest rate is very high for the risk run by the lender; if the terms were not fully explained to you at the outset; or if you were pressured into signing the agreement. You should consider getting advice about this from a solicitor paid for under the Legal Aid Scheme (see Appendix 6).

In Scotland, while you can obtain a time order to reschedule the debt, the court does not have the power to prevent the lender from obtaining possession.

CHAPTER SEVEN

Repairs and improvements

The need for repairs to your home can be a serious worry when you are trying to make ends meet on a tight budget. Similarly, there may be improvements you wish to make to your home which would make life a lot easier, if only you could afford them. It is important to check whether you are, in fact, responsible for the repairs you need to do. In some cases, you may not be responsible at all, or you may share responsibility with others. This applies especially to flat owners and other leaseholders. In this chapter we outline your rights as a leaseholder, and detail the various ways you can try to raise the money to pay for any work for which you are responsible.

GRANTS FROM THE LOCAL AUTHORITY

In 1990 a new grant system was introduced by the Local Government and Housing Act 1989. This Act contains a number of different measures to help with repairs and improvements and to provide for the needs of disabled people. The local housing authority is responsible for administering grants. In Scotland, repairs grants are made under the Housing (Scotland) Act 1987. The principal types of grants are:

- ☐ renovation grants;
- ☐ common parts grant;
- ☐ Houses in multiple occupation (HMO) grants;
- ☐ disabled facilities grant.

You will not be able to apply for one of these grants, other than a disabled facilities grant, if your house was built or converted less than ten years ago. For more details about house renovation grants generally you should read Department of Environment Circular 12/90 or the leaflet House Renovation Grants (see Appendix 9). In Scotland, a similar grant, called a 'disabled persons improvement grant', may be available. Contact your local district council.

Renovation grants

You can get a renovation grant to pay for repairs and/or improvements to your home. The local authority must give you a grant if your home is 'unfit for human habitation' and they feel that renovation is the most satisfactory course of action for dealing with the building. If this is the case, then you are entitled to a grant to make your home fit for human habitation. However, eligibility and the amount of any grant will depend on your financial position.

If your home is not unfit for human habitation, then a renovation grant can be made at the discretion of the local authority. In Scotland, home improvement grants or repairs grants may be available for standard amenities.

Common parts grant

A common parts grant is for repairs or improvements to the common parts of buildings that are divided into flats – for example, the roof and common hall and staircase. Either the owner of the building or a number of the tenants/leaseholders of the building acting together may apply for this grant. Such a grant will be made at the discretion of the local authority.

There are complicated rules about the calculation of the amount of the grant payable to tenants/leaseholders who apply together.

House in multiple occupation (HMO) grants

Only landlords of houses in multiple occupation where the occupiers do not have their own self-contained accommodation can apply for these grants to repair and improve the property.

Disabled facilities grants

You can get a disabled facilities grant if you need to make adaptations to a building or need to provide facilities in a property, for the benefit of a disabled person. This can extend to work on the common parts of a building if this is necessary. Works to improve access to and within the home of a disabled person will generally attract a mandatory grant from the local authority as will work to improve facilities – for example, cooking and heating to meet the needs of a disabled person. The cost of other types of improvement to help a disabled occupier is at the discretion of the authority. Full details are contained in Department of Environment Circular 10/90 (see Appendix 9 for how to obtain Department of Environment circulars).

OTHER HELP FROM LOCAL AUTHORITIES

Group repair schemes

Group repair schemes are arranged by local authorities who undertake external repairs to a number of houses all at one time. These will normally be a row of terraced houses, all of which are in poor repair and, in the main, privately owned. These schemes used to be called 'envelope' schemes.

You cannot force a local authority to include your home in one of these schemes but it may be worth asking about such a scheme. You can be asked to contribute towards the cost of the work and the amount that you have to pay will depend on your financial position.

Minor works assistance

With minor works assistance, you may be able to get help from the local authority with the cost of the following:

- ☐ providing or improving the thermal insulation of a house or flat;
- ☐ repairs to a house which the local authority has included in a clearance area for demolition in due course;
- ☐ repairs, improvements or adaptations to a property where the occupier is 60 years of age or more; *or*
- ☐ adaptations to a house or flat to enable a person aged 60 or more to come to live with you to be cared for.

The maximum help at any one time is £1,080 per application and £3,240 in any three-year period. This scheme is only available if you receive income support (see page 28), housing benefit (see page 24), family credit (see page 14), disability working allowance (see page 19) or council tax benefit (see page 55). Further advice is contained in Department of Environment Circular 4/90 (see Appendix 9).

APPLYING FOR LOCAL AUTHORITY GRANTS

You must first apply to your local authority grants section. This may be part of the housing department or possibly the environmental health department. Check with the town hall to find out where to apply. If the local authority thinks you qualify for a grant, you will have to fill in an application form and someone from the local authority will come to inspect your home.

Occasionally the local authority may inspect first if there is any doubt about the work required. After the inspection, the local authority will let you know what work is required and, if there are to be major alterations, they may ask you to have plans drawn up. You will have to pay for these yourself before you know whether or not you are eligible for a grant. If you are successful in getting a local authority grant, you can claim back the amount you spent on fees for plans, etc, as part of your costs.

The purpose of giving a grant is to help people put their homes into good repair. The local authority, therefore, may ask for a lot more work to be done than you had planned. In some circumstances, you may have to do some extra work to get your grant, but in other cases the local authority has the discretion to accept more limited standards of improvement. They may use this discretion if, for example, there is an elderly or ill person in the house who would find the upheaval too much, or if you could not raise enough money to finance the full works stipulated. Discuss this with your local authority.

Once you and the local authority have agreed on the work to be done, you will have to get at least two estimates of the cost of the work and submit them to the local authority. Some local authorities provide a list of local builders you can use, otherwise you will have to find one yourself. Once all this has been done, the local authority will decide whether or not to approve your grant. *You must never start work on your home before you have had official approval or you could lose any chance of a grant.*

If you are refused a grant you have the right to written reasons for the refusal and you could try appealing to a local councillor to see if the local authority will change its mind. Sometimes local authorities run out of money for grants so, if you can, it is best to get your application in near the beginning of the financial year (April). If you are refused a grant because there is no money left, apply again in the new financial year.

There are a number of different types of grants available **in Scotland** including:

☐ lead pipe replacement grants; *and*

☐ improvement grants for electrical work.

In addition, there is a care and repair scheme aimed primarily at the elderly.

How much will the grant be for?

If you are awarded a grant by the local authority you may be expected to pay something towards the total cost of the building works. Whether you have to make a contribution depends on your financial position. The local authority will want details of your savings and income. The basis of the calculation is that if your income exceeds your needs, as defined by the government, then the grant will be reduced by the amount of a notional 'affordable' loan you are assumed to be able to raise and repay out of this excess.

The 'affordable' loan calculation

The amount of the 'affordable' loan depends on your income, your savings and the number and types of people in your household. The calculation works by comparing your net income with the **applicable amount** (see page 31) for your family. If your income is the same or less than your applicable amount, there is no deduction from the grant and you will receive all the costs of the building works. If your income is calculated at more than your applicable amount, then your 'affordable loan' is calculated by multiplying the excess by a prescribed figure (known as the multiplier). The result is the sum to be deducted from your grant.

Example
Mr and Mrs Khan have one child aged 10. They have no savings. The costs of works to their house which they jointly own has been approved for grant aid at £12,000. Their applicable amount, based on April 1994 rates, is:

	£ p
Personal allowance for a couple	£71.70
Personal allowance for a child aged 10	£15.65
Family premium	£10.05
Grant premium	£40.00
Total income	£137.40

Their income is £180 net earnings per week plus child benefit of £10.20 which totals £190.20. The excess of income over the applicable amount is £198.20 - £137.40 = £52.80. The grant payable will be reduced by £52.80 x 35.52 (the multiplier – see table below to find this) = £1,875.46. The grant which Mr and Mrs Khan will receive is £12,000 - £1,875.46 = £10,124.54.

Which multiplier to use in calculating affordable loans

Difference between income and applicable amount	*Multiplier*
less than £47.95	17.76
£47.95 to £95.89	35.52
£95.89 to £191.78	142.06
more than £191.78	355.15

There are a number of points which need to be noted:

- Since April 1994, the maximum grant payable has been £20,000.

- Average weekly income is generally calculated based on net income received during the 52 weeks prior to the grant application. But if another period more accurately reflects your current financial situation, then this should be used instead.

- Savings over £5,000 are taken to produce weekly income at the rate of £1 per week for every £250 over £5,000. There is no upper limit for savings.

- In addition to the types of premium applied in calculating housing benefit and council tax benefit (see Chapter four and Appendix 3) there is a special grant premium of £40 per week.

- Applicants in receipt of income support will qualify for 100 per cent grant aid.

- The affordable loan sum deducted from the grant to be paid is not dependent on you actually being able to raise a loan.

- In the case of disabled facilities grants, the financial resources of the disabled person are taken into account in calculating the affordable loan.

GRANTS FROM THE HOME ENERGY EFFICIENCY SCHEME

The Home Energy Efficiency Scheme (HEES) can provide grants to help with the cost of loft insulation, draught-proofing and energy advice. You can apply for a HEES grant if:

- you get income support, family credit, disability working allowance, housing benefit, council tax benefit or disability living allowance; *or*

- you are aged 60 or over; *and*

- you (or the person you live with as husband or wife) own or rent your home.

You will get the full cost of the works up to a maximum of:

For loft insulation	£189.70
For draught-proofing	£128.50
For loft insulation and draught-proofing	£305.00
For energy advice (only if you also have draught-proofing or loft insulation)	£10.00

HEES grants are administered by the Energy Action Grants Agency (EAGA) (see Appendix 7). The work must be done by an organisation registered with EAGA, or by yourself, in which case the grant can be paid direct to you.

LOANS FROM OTHER SOURCES

If you do not succeed in getting a grant for repairs and improvements, you may be able to get a loan from other sources – for example, a bank, building society, or a reputable finance company – to pay for the work. Even if you do qualify for a local authority grant, it is likely you will still have to raise a loan for the part of the work not met by the amount awarded.

Loans taken out before 6 April 1988 for the purposes of home improvements will be eligible for tax relief. However, if you change the loan, by, for example, refinancing, you will lose the tax relief. Loans taken out for repairs, or any loans taken out after 6 April 1988 are no longer eligible for tax relief.

It may be possible to get an interest-free loan or community care grant from the social fund to meet the cost of some minor repairs and improvements (see page 50).

How much will a loan cost?

Raising an extra loan on top of your mortgage will not necessarily cost you much more each month. For example, if you had a £20,000 loan over 25 years, and were paying interest on it at 8 per cent, the monthly net repayment would be £135.40. An extra £3,000 borrowed to meet repairs spread out over the same period of time would cost you an additional £23.43 per month without tax relief. Appendix 1 shows you how to work out how much your loan would cost.

How will you pay for a loan?

If you are receiving income support

The Benefits Agency will increase your benefit to cover some or all of the interest payable on any loan you manage to get for major repairs necessary to maintain the fabric of your home or for the following improvements:

- [ ] putting in bathroom fixtures – for example, a washbasin, bath, shower or toilet;
- [ ] damp-proofing;
- [ ] providing or improving ventilation or natural light;

- [ ] providing or improving drainage facilities;
- [ ] putting in electric lighting and sockets;
- [ ] putting in heating, including central heating;
- [ ] putting in storage facilities for fuel and refuse;
- [ ] improving the structural condition of the home;
- [ ] improving facilities for storing, preparing and cooking food;
- [ ] insulation;
- [ ] work to create separate sleeping accommodation for a boy and girl both aged ten or over.

The Benefits Agency may assist with any survey fees you have to pay while trying to arrange the loan through the social fund community care grants or budgeting loans schemes.

If you are not receiving income support

You will need to make sure that your income is enough to meet the increased payments. (See Chapter two and Chapter four for ways of maximising your income.) You will also want to make sure that your loan is arranged on the cheapest possible basis (see Chapter five for more information). Your lender will calculate how much you are able to borrow on the basis of your total income.

How to get a loan

You should approach your present lender first. If you have an expensive endowment mortgage or a loan from a finance company, you may wish to rearrange all your loans on a cheaper basis with a building society, bank or local authority. (See Chapter five for more information.)

Your lender will look at the work required and its costs, your income and your property. Normally the property will be valued (you will have to pay for this) before your lender decides whether to give you a loan. There will be some legal and administrative fees involved in granting a second loan, so check with your lender how much these will be. You can try asking your lender to include the fees as part of the loan.

If you are refused a loan by your present lender, you will have to look for alternative sources of money – the obvious first alternative being a bank.

Wherever you go to borrow the additional money, check the details of the loan very carefully. Some short-term bank loans (up to five years) are charged at quite a high interest rate so are to be avoided. It is always the case that the shorter the repayment period the higher the monthly cost, so always try to get your loan over the longest possible term – 20-25 years if you can.

Negotiating with your lender

First you will have to find out how much you need to borrow. Then you will have to show your lender how you will meet the payments. Write to your lender giving details of:

- ☐ estimates of the cost of the work (send a copy of your original estimate);
- ☐ any grant you will be getting from your local authority (or say that you are applying and will send further information later);
- ☐ how much you are likely to need to borrow.

Then you will need to show how you will meet the payments.

If you are receiving income support

- ☐ Send a letter from your Benefits Agency office confirming that they are prepared in principle to meet the interest on the additional payments, whether in whole or in part.
- ☐ Explain either the way in which you can meet the capital/insurance premium that the Benefits Agency will not pay (see Chapter two and Chapter four for ways to increase your income to do this), *or* that you would like the lender to waive the capital part of the mortgage until you are in a position to start paying it. Give some idea of how and when this might be.

See Appendix 5 for an example of a letter to send to your lender.

If you are not receiving income support

- ☐ Give details of your income, and what it comprises. If your income is likely to increase in the near future, say so. (See Chapter two for ways of increasing your income);
- ☐ Show how you will be able to meet the payments on the loan, as well as your other outgoings. You can do this by listing your outgoings in detail, and showing the money you have left over once those commitments are paid.

See Appendix 5 for an example of a letter to send to your lender.

RESPONSIBILITY FOR REPAIRS IF YOU ARE A LEASEHOLDER

In England and Wales, there is an important distinction between property held by leasehold, and property held by freehold. This distinction does not apply in Scotland where a 'feudal' land-holding system still exists.

If you bought your property as a leaseholder, your lease will set out who is responsible for repairing the property. Often, the lease will provide that the freeholder is responsible for structural repairs and maintenance to the property – for example, to the walls and roof – and the leaseholder is responsible for the internal repairs and decoration. When the freeholder carries out repairs and maintenance, the cost of this work is passed on to the leaseholder through the annual service charge.

Freeholders can only recover the cost of repairs through the service charge if these are specified in the lease. In addition, the Landlord and Tenant Acts of 1985 and 1987 place certain limitations on the amount of service charges that can be lawfully recovered from you. The Landlord and Tenant Act 1985 specifies that costs which are incurred when providing a service are recoverable only if they are reasonable or the services or works are of a reasonable standard. In addition, if major works are proposed the freeholder must follow a particular procedure if s/he wishes to recover the cost of major works from the leaseholders (see below). The Leasehold Reform, Housing and Urban Development Act 1993 (referred to in this chapter as the 1993 Act), now gives leaseholders the right to have service charges independently audited.

Where a tenant has exercised the 'right to buy'

The Housing Act 1985 (and the Housing (Scotland) Act 1987) imposes limitations on the amount that can be recovered in service charges from tenants who have bought their flats from a public sector landlord under the **right to buy** legislation.

When a tenant's claim to exercise the right to buy is established, the landlord must serve a notice stating the purchase price, and must give estimates of the service charges which the tenant will be asked to pay under the lease for an initial specified period (usually five years). The liability to pay these service charges will, in certain cases, be limited to the amount of the estimates. You cannot get housing benefit to cover these charges but you can sometimes get income support to meet the interest on loans taken out to pay them (see page 32).

Major works and consultation

The Landlord and Tenant Acts provide that leaseholders and their recognised tenants' associations must be consulted whenever major works are proposed. Major works are defined as works costing above the limit of £50 per flat or £1,000 in total, whichever is the greater. If the freeholder, or her/his agent, fails to comply with the consultation procedure detailed below and fails to persuade a court that the procedure is not necessary, then all that s/he can recover from a leaseholder, for works carried out on or after 1 September 1988, is the greater of £50 per flat or £1,000 in total.

If the freeholder proposes to carry out major works, s/he must follow the consultation procedure outlined below.

The procedure for consultation

If there is a tenants' or residents' association, the freeholder must send the secretary of the association a notice containing a detailed specification of the works to be carried out. The notice must give a reasonable time for the association to suggest from whom estimates should be obtained. The freeholder does not have to accept the suggestions.

The freeholder must obtain two estimates for the work, one of which must be from a person wholly unconnected with the freeholder. The estimates must be sent to the secretary of the tenants' or residents' association.

The freeholder must also send each of the leaseholders represented by the association and affected by the works a notice briefly describing the works and summarising the estimates. The notice must explain that the leaseholders have the right to inspect and take copies of the work specifications and the estimates. The notice must also ask for comments to be sent to a specified address within a period of not less than one month.

If there is no tenants' or residents' association, the freeholder must either send the notice to each leaseholder or display it where all the leaseholders are likely to see it.

Unless the repairs are urgent, they must not begin until the time given by the freeholder for comments has run out.

If a freeholder or her/his agent has not complied with this procedure, s/he can only recover more than £50 per flat or £1,000 in total if s/he has persuaded a court that s/he has acted reasonably.

Grant-aided works

Where works have been paid for with the assistance of a local authority grant, the amount of the grant must be deducted from the cost of works to establish the amount that can be lawfully recovered from leaseholders in service charges.

Demands for service charges

The Landlord and Tenant Acts provide that written demands for service charges must contain the freeholder's name and address. If they do not, the service charge is not payable until this information is given. In addition, service charges need not be paid until the freeholder provides an address for the service of notices on her/him.

Late demands

The Landlord and Tenant Acts state that, if a bill for a service charge is sent out and the works were carried out more than 18 months before, then the cost of the work can only be recovered lawfully if, during the 18-month period, the freeholder sent written notice saying the costs had been incurred and the bill would be forthcoming.

Challenging demands for service charges

If you want to challenge a demand for service charges, it is important that all the leaseholders act together, preferably through a residents' or tenants' association. Keep copies of all correspondence sent and received and also keep a record of services both provided and not provided. All complaints should be made in writing and be dated. You should keep copies of all complaints to show that the freeholder had been notified when, for example, s/he failed to provide a service or the standard of service was inadequate.

If the freeholder fails to comply with a request to provide information to which leaseholders have a right, then you can ask for a court order. This will compel the freeholder to comply with the lease by providing the information you need. If your freeholder is a local authority, then you can also complain to a local councillor or to the Ombudsman if the authority still fails to comply with a request for information.

If it is clear from the figures provided that the demand for service charges is unreasonable, you could try negotiating with the freeholder for a more reasonable figure. You may need an independent expert's opinion, or alternative estimates to help in your negotiations. If you have decided to withhold part of the service charge and pay only what you consider is reasonable, it is wise to supply independent evidence to justify the amount you have paid.

If negotiations are not successful, the freeholder can either start proceedings to recover the outstanding charge, or you may start proceedings for a declaration that the demand is based upon:

- ☐ relevant costs (specified in the lease) which are not reasonable; *or*
- ☐ works or services which are not of a reasonable standard; *or*
- ☐ works that fall outside the scope of the lease.

Appointing an auditor

The 1993 Act provides that two-thirds or more of the leaseholders in a property can appoint a qualified accountant or surveyor to act as an auditor to examine whether the management of the property and expenditure of service charges is efficient and effective. The auditor has the power to request information and be shown documents by the landlord and any other person. This includes not only the information you can ask for under the Landlord and Tenant Acts but also any other documents reasonably required for the audit.

This power is helpful if your tenants' association can afford to employ an accountant or surveyor to act on its behalf or can get one to act for free (the auditor cannot be a tenant of the property).

Forfeiture for arrears of service charges

Most leases state that the lease can be forfeited if the rent or service charges are in arrears or if the leaseholder has breached a clause in the lease. **Forfeit** is the legal word which is used when a freeholder brings a lease to an end before it would normally expire. All leases contain a clause stating that the freeholder is entitled to 're-enter' the property and forfeit the lease in certain situations.

Even though most leases allow the freeholder to 're-enter forthwith' (immediately), it would be a criminal offence to do this if anyone was living there. The freeholder must go to court and obtain an order to end the lease. If the freeholder claims possession for arrears of rent or similar charges, a formal demand for the money due must be made, unless the lease specifically states that the lease can be forfeited whether or not the charges are formally demanded, which is common.

If possession is claimed on other grounds, formal notice must be given telling the leaseholder that a clause in the lease has been breached, giving the leaseholder an opportunity to put matters right. If proceedings are brought for arrears of rent or service charges, the proceedings are automatically stopped if all money due, including the freeholder's legal costs, is paid to the court at least five days before the hearing.

If the freeholder is claiming forfeiture because of arrears of service charges which are in dispute, you should apply for **relief against forfeiture** at the court hearing. You should explain that you are not in breach of your lease and ask the court to decide whether the charges are reasonable. You will need to provide, as evidence, copies of all correspondence, independent experts' opinions and alternative estimates.

Even after a court hearing to forfeit a lease, a leaseholder still has four weeks to pay all the money due (including the freeholder's legal costs). If the money is paid within this time limit, the lease continues as before. If the money is not paid within this time, the lease is brought to an end and the leaseholder can be evicted.

If the freeholder goes to court for breach of any other clause in the lease, the court has wide discretion to grant relief from forfeiture and stop the lease from being brought to an end. This is normally done if the leaseholder has stopped breaking the terms of the lease and promises not to break them in the future. It used to be assumed that relief from forfeiture could only be sought during proceedings brought by the freeholder. However, it has now been established, in a judgment from the House of Lords, that, if a freeholder has obtained forfeiture and has re-entered the property by serving a formal notice but without taking court proceedings, the leaseholder can apply to a court for relief against forfeiture.

Buying the freehold

There are now three ways in which tenants can buy the freehold of their property:

- ☐ You have the right of first refusal if the landlord wishes to sell the freehold.
- ☐ You can apply to the county court to force the landlord to sell the freehold if s/he is in breach of her/his obligations under the lease.
- ☐ You can now exercise the right to 'collective enfranchisement' and purchase the freehold whether or not the landlord is in breach of her/his obligations.

Right of first refusal

Under the Landlord and Tenant Act 1987, leaseholders of a property have the right to buy the freehold themselves if the freeholder wants to sell it. This is called the right of first refusal. If this right is ignored by the freeholder, the leaseholders can require that the new freeholder sells the freehold to them at the same price. If the leaseholders are not sure whether they want to buy the freehold, the Act allows them to delay a new landlord taking over the property for at least four months, without penalty, while they consider whether they wish to buy the freehold after all.

Who qualifies?
Leaseholders who have the right of first refusal are called **qualifying tenants**. A leaseholder who owns at least three flats in the building, or occupies her/his flat for business purposes cannot be a qualifying tenant.

Leaseholders who own fewer than three flats in the building are qualifying tenants.

In order for leaseholders to exercise the right of first refusal, more than half of the flats in the building must be occupied by qualifying tenants. Some non-owning occupiers may also be qualifying tenants if they moved in before 15 January 1989 and have security of tenure.

Some landlords are not required to offer leaseholders the right of first refusal. These include local authorities, housing associations and other public sector landlords. A resident landlord who has lived in a flat in a converted building, using it as her/his only or main home for at least a year, is also outside the Act.

How does it work?
There are three stages to the procedure:

☐ The freeholder must first offer to sell her/his interest in the property to the qualifying tenants by giving them written notice of the terms of the sale (including the price).

☐ The qualifying tenants then have at least two months after receiving notice to decide how to respond. They can accept the offer; reject it and put forward a counter offer; or simply not accept it. Acceptance of an offer or counter offer must be supported by a majority of the qualifying tenants for it to be legally effective. If the landlord rejects a counter offer, you can negotiate. If a sale is agreed, you will have at least four months after receiving notice to decide who should buy the landlord's interest on everyone's behalf.

☐ Even if a sale is agreed, either side can withdraw at any time up until signing a formal contract. In certain circumstances, you may then have to pay the landlord's legal costs. If a sale is not agreed, or if you do not choose a purchaser in the time allowed by the landlord, the landlord is free to sell. However, s/he can only sell the freehold during the following 12 months and the sale price must be no lower than the price at which the freehold was offered to you.

Compulsory acquisition of freehold

If you feel that your freeholder has not fulfilled the repair or other duties of the lease, the Landlord and Tenant Act 1987 also allows two-thirds of the qualifying leaseholders to apply at any time to the county court for an order compelling the landlord to sell the freehold to them. The judge will only grant this order if you can show that the landlord has been in breach of her/his duties to you, the leaseholders, and that it would not be sufficient for the court to appoint a manager to carry out these duties on her/his behalf.

Collective enfranchisement

The 1993 Act gives leaseholders a new, wider power to purchase the freehold, known as **collective enfranchisement**.

Who qualifies?
Before leaseholders have a right to collective enfranchisement, certain conditions must be met:

- [ ] the freehold must be of self-contained premises;
- [ ] not more than 10 per cent of the property can be used for non-residential purposes;
- [ ] if the property is not a purpose-built block of flats, and the landlord or an adult member of his family has occupied part of it as her/his principal home for 12 months, the freehold cannot be bought by collective enfranchisement;
- [ ] the property must not be designated as exempted from inheritance tax by the Inland Revenue;
- [ ] the property must not be owned by the National Trust or the Crown (although the government has undertaken to allow most Crown leaseholders equivalent rights to enfranchisement);
- [ ] the participating leaseholders must own two or more flats which must not be less than two-thirds of the total number of qualifying flats in the premises, and not less than half the total number of flats in the premises;
- [ ] at least half the leaseholders wishing to buy the freehold must have been resident in the property either in the last 12 months or for three out of the last ten years.

How does it work?
Preliminary enquiries: The 1993 Act gives you the right to obtain certain information from the freeholder, her/his agents, and other relevant people, including:

- [ ] information about the ownership of the freehold and leaseholds of the premises and other matters, such as the level of service charges;
- [ ] the result of a survey or other report and whether an application for collective enfranchisement has already been made.

This information will help you and other leaseholders to establish whether you meet the conditions for collective enfranchisement and with whom you will have to negotiate. It will also be of help in establishing the price which you should offer for the freehold.

Before you can make an application to buy the freehold, you must also appoint a **nominee purchaser** to act on your behalf in negotiations with the freeholders. The nominee purchaser is the person or people to whom the landlord will sell the freehold. Often this will be a limited company set up jointly by the tenants of the property to purchase and manage it. But it could also be an officer or officers of your tenants' association or anyone else you choose. You should also obtain a valuation of the freehold from a surveyor with knowledge of the local market, on which to base your purchase offer.

Notice of claim: Very often, at this stage, the freeholder, in the knowledge that you have a right to purchase the freehold, will make an offer to sell and you can begin to negotiate with her/him. But if s/he does not and you still wish to buy the freehold, you should now give the freeholder an **initial notice** of your claim to exercise the right of enfranchisement.

The notice must be signed by all the participating tenants and should set out the full particulars of the freehold you wish to buy; the basis on which you believe you have right to purchase the freehold and the price which you are offering. The notice must be accompanied by a plan of the premises and should give a time limit (of at least two months) for the freeholder to reply by issuing a counter notice.

Negotiations and purchase: The leaseholders and the freeholder have two months from the date of the counter notice in which to agree a purchase price and any other conditions of the sale.

If, after two months, agreement has not been reached, either party may refer the issue to the Leasehold Valuation Tribunal within six months of the counter notice. The Tribunal has the power to make a decision which will be binding on both parties. This valuation will be based on the 'marriage value'

– that is, the increased value of the freehold and leasehold when they have the same owner – and calculated using a formula set out in Schedule 6 of the Act. If, having issued the initial notice, you decide not to proceed you may be liable for your freeholder's costs.

Some leaseholders are in fact sub-tenants of other parties who hold leases from the freeholder of the property. If this applies to you, as well as purchasing the freehold, you will need to buy out the intermediate leaseholder(s) as well. All the rights and procedures outlined above also apply to these negotiations.

The enfranchisement process was only introduced in November 1993 and is relatively complicated. Initial indications are that fewer leaseholders have taken advantage of it than was originally envisaged. The government proposes to extend further the rights of leaseholders through a new form of tenure known as **commonhold** and will probably introduce legislation to implement this in the 1994/95 session of parliament. You can obtain further advice on leasehold enfranchisement from the Leasehold Enfranchisement Advisory Service (see Appendix 7). This service can also advise you on other rights you might have – for example, how to extend your lease under the 1993 Act.

Homeowners' right to buy leases

If you own a house, but someone else owns the freehold of the land it is built on, you can buy the freehold under the Leasehold Reform Act 1967, if the leasehold is for more than 21 years and it has been your home for a minimum of three years.

Separation

If you and your partner are separating, it is advisable to see a solicitor to help you negotiate what your share in the home will be, bearing in mind that you may have to go to court. Make sure, however, that the solicitor is an expert in this area (see Appendix 7). You may well also need advice about your benefit entitlement from one of the organisations listed in Appendix 7. This section explains how you can try to keep your home in the long term and how to make sure that you do not lose it before a final settlement is made.

INTRODUCTION

If you are married or you jointly own your home with someone else:

- *you do not have to leave your home* unless your partner gets a court order which rules that you should leave, or the lender obtains a court order for possession;
- *never agree to the sale of your home* until you have looked at all the possible options. If you are getting advice from a solicitor or advice centre, they may not be aware of the many ways of increasing your income (see Chapters two, three and four) or reducing your housing costs (see Chapter five) which might enable you to keep your home. If you are not happy with the advice you have been given, get a second opinion and ask for an explanation of anything you do not understand;
- *act quickly*. The longer you leave doing anything about your home and mortgage, the more difficult it will be to keep it;
- *do not be put off by the thought of high legal costs*. You may get legal aid and have to pay nothing at all, although you should ask your solicitor to explain about the statutory charge (see Appendix 6).

If you are not married, and you do not own a share in the home, your rights are very much more limited, but you should not do anything without first getting advice. Also, see pages 104 and 109.

WHAT TO DO IN THE SHORT TERM

Until a final agreement has been made which decides the property rights you and your partner have, you must decide where you want to live, and try to ensure that, if the house is not in your name, your partner does not borrow money against the property or sell your home without telling you. You should not sign any document without first obtaining advice and being sure you understand the consequences.

Should you stay?

If you are married or own the home solely or jointly with your partner, you normally have the right to stay in the short term, but you may not want to do this. The possibilities open to you are outlined below:

- ☐ If your partner is happy to leave, you can obviously stay in your home, but you must make sure that the mortgage and other payments are being kept up. See page 115 for what to do if you are taking over this responsibility.

- ☐ If you both want to remain in the home, you can both try to stay there until a property settlement has been agreed. If this is not possible, you can try to get your partner out by taking legal action. Your legal rights, and how quickly you can enforce them, depend very much on whether you are married to your partner, on who owns the property and on how your partner has behaved towards you and your children if you have any.

If you are not married and do not own a share, see below and page 109.

If there has been violence or harassment

Note: The Acts mentioned in this section apply equally to women and men. However, as it is normally women who need to apply for protection using this legislation, this section has been written from their point of view.

If you are not married and your partner owns the home (or you own it jointly) you will only be able to force him to leave if he has behaved violently, or in such a way as to have caused distress to you and/or the children. You will have to provide evidence of this. You can seek an *injunction* under the Domestic Violence and Matrimonial Proceedings Act 1976 in any county court. The injunction can order your partner not to 'molest' you or any children living with you (this is called a 'non-molestation order'), and can exclude him from the home or a specified area around it (an 'ouster order'). 'Molesting' means being violent, but also includes pestering or harassing you. If you have been forced to leave, the injunction can order your partner to let you return. Note that ouster orders are sometimes granted for a limited period – three or six months – in the first instance. In Scotland, you will need to apply to the Sheriff Court for a declarator of occupancy rights in terms of the Matrimonial Homes (Family Protection) (Scotland) Act 1981 and *then* seek an 'exclusion order' and/or an 'interdict' to prevent the former partner molesting you or the children. In England and Wales, you can also apply for an injunction under the Children Act 1989.

If you are married to your partner, your rights to exclude him are much more extensive:

- ☐ You can apply for an injunction under the 1976 Act just as an unmarried woman can in the circumstances described above. In Scotland, if you are not joint owner or tenant you have occupancy rights as the 'non-entitled spouse'. You can seek a declaration of this right in the Sheriff Court. You can also seek exclusions and an interdict in the circumstances described below.

- ☐ You can apply for (i) a 'personal protection order' and (ii) an 'exclusion order' in the Magistrates' Court under the Domestic Proceedings and Magistrates' Courts Act 1978. However, to obtain a personal protection order you must establish actual or threatened violence against you or a child, and to obtain an exclusion order you must establish actual violence. Moreover, the orders that can be made are more limited than those under the 1976 Act. The court procedure, however, is simpler than that under the 1976 Act. In Scotland, under s4 of the Matrimonial Homes Act 1981, you can seek an exclusion order if it is necessary for your protection or the protection of any children.

- ☐ A spouse has the right to occupy (and make payments on) the matrimonial home even if it is in the other spouse's name. These rights are given by the Matrimonial Homes Act 1983 and the 1981 Act in Scotland. In addition, the Act gives the court power to exclude either spouse from the matrimonial home. In deciding whether to grant the order, the court will look at the conduct of the parties, their respective needs and financial resources, the needs of any children and other relevant factors. An application under the Matrimonial Homes Act will normally be made where divorce or judicial separation proceedings have already started, although this is not always essential. However, if in addition to an ouster order you wish to obtain a non-molestation order to protect you and/or your children, you *will* have to start proceedings for divorce or judicial separation if you have not already done so. In Scotland, the equivalent is an *interdict* under the 1981 Act. S14(2) prohibits a spouse from entering the matrimonial home. S14(2)(b) bars the spouse from the home. S14(2)(a) provides a non-molestation interdict.

- [ ] You can apply for a non-molestation or an ouster injunction (or the Scottish equivalents) if you have started divorce or judicial separation proceedings.

- [ ] You can apply for an injunction in proceedings taken under the Children Act 1989.

As you can see, the law in this area is rather complicated and it will be essential for you to obtain legal advice as to the best course of action.

Although you may have a long-term right to remain in your home and intend to pursue that right, injunctions are not always obeyed, and you may have to leave your home anyway and find somewhere else to stay while an injunction is being arranged. The choices open to you are limited:

- [ ] **You can ask your local authority for temporary accommodation** under the Housing Act 1985 Part III or the Housing (Scotland) Act 1987. This says that local authorities have a duty to find accommodation for anyone with dependent children who has become homeless because of violence or the threat of it from someone living in the home. You may be asked for evidence of the violence – for example, from a doctor or health visitor. If there is no evidence, the local authority may not help you as they may say that you can continue to live in your home. If the local authority gives you temporary accommodation, they may try to insist that you should apply for an injunction to make your home 'safe' to return to. You do not have to do this, but you will need help to argue with the local authority, which you can get from a housing advice centre, SHAC, a Women's Aid Refuge, a solicitor, or a local advice centre (see Appendix 7). Note that the government is planning to make changes to the homelessness legislation (see page 140), but these should not affect your right to temporary accommodation.

- [ ] **You can go and stay with friends or relatives.** But, if this arrangement can only last for a few days, you will probably find yourself in the position outlined in the previous paragraph.

- [ ] **You can go to a Women's Aid Refuge.** Any woman can go to a refuge for advice. Refuges can also provide accommodation for women at risk of violence and their children. Their addresses are kept confidential to protect the women living there, but you can contact them through the Women's Aid Federation, citizens advice bureaux, social services departments, SHAC or the police (see Appendix 7). If you have to leave your home for fear of domestic violence, you can continue to claim income support towards the mortgage interest, as well as the mortgage interest on your present home (see page 33).

Note that, if you leave the home you own, or jointly own, because of a breakdown in your relationship, the Benefits Agency and the local authority will ignore your share of the value of the house for at least 26 weeks in working out how much capital you have for benefit purposes. If you make efforts to sell the home, or take legal action to allow you to move back in, then it can be ignored for longer; see Appendix 4 for more details.

Preventing the sale of your home or a reduction of your share in it

Whether you are living in your home or not, it is vital to take all possible steps to protect your rights to live in the home and to your share in the value of the home by making sure that your partner does not try to raise another mortgage or sell your home without telling you. Do not sign any documents without getting advice from your own solicitor. If your partner does raise another mortgage, that is, he borrows on the security of the home, this will inevitably reduce the value of the equity, and may also increase the risk of lenders applying for repossession of the home if your partner defaults on the additional payments.

If the mortgage(s) are in your partner's name and he has left and you continue to live in the home and claim income support, you can claim for mortgage interest to cover all loans charged to the property irrespective of why they were taken out. Whether you are married or not, you can claim for these payments if your partner either cannot or will not meet the payments and it is necessary for you to pay them in order to stay in the home (see page 32). Note that the DSS says that the new rules restricting the payment of increased mortgage interest if you were already on income support (see page 37) should not apply in this situation.

If you are married

If the property is in both names, neither of you can sell or borrow money without the other's signature. However, to avoid any possibility of your signature being used without your consent, it may be as well to request that all your documents are dealt with via your solicitor if you have one. If you do sign any documents without getting your own legal advice and the lender later brings possession proceedings, you should immediately get legal advice (see Appendix 6). In England and Wales, at least, you may have a defence if your husband (or partner, if you are not married) put unfair pressure on you or misled you (see page 78).

Registering a charge
In England and Wales, if the property is in your spouse's sole name, you will have to 'register a charge' to show that you are claiming an interest in the property. This, in effect, stops the property being sold because your interest overrides any transactions made after your charge has been registered. You can get your solicitor to do this, and help under the green form scheme is available (see Appendix 6), but registering a charge is quite simple and you can do it yourself. Note that an *existing* lender will be able to sell the property if there are arrears, but you may be able to negotiate to take over the mortgage yourself (see page 116). If your husband owns more than one property, you can only register a charge on the one you have been living in.

In England, you will need to buy Land Registry Form No 96 at a law stationers. This is relatively inexpensive. Law stationers are listed in the Yellow Pages. Fill in the form and write across the top: 'This search is being made for the purpose of the Matrimonial Homes Act 1983.' Post it to your District Land Registry Office. The Central Land Registry (Lincoln's Inn Fields, London WC2, 071-917 8888), publishes an address list of District Land Registry offices and the areas they cover. They will tell you if your home is registered at the Land Registry and what the Title Number is.

- **If your home is registered:** buy and complete Land Registry Form 99 and send it to the Chief Land Registrar at the same District Land Registry Office as before. There is no fee.

- **If your home is not registered (unregistered):** you will have to register a Class F Charge at the Land Charges Registry. Again, all you will have to do is complete a form. Buy Land Charges Form K2, complete it and post it to the Land Charges Department, Burrington Way, Plymouth. The fee is £1. This will register a charge on the property.

In Scotland, because of the provisions of the Blank Bonds and Trusts Act 1696 it is not generally possible for a wife to obtain an interest in the matrimonial home if the title is in the husband's sole name. There are some exceptions – for example, in the case of fraud, legal advice should be sought.

If you are divorcing

If you divorce, and the court makes an order allowing you to continue to live in the matrimonial home and the property is still in your husband's name, you must renew your registration (see page 108) as soon as possible. Your solicitor should do this for you, or you can buy, complete and send either Land Registry Form 100 (if the land is registered) or Land Charges form K7 (if the land is unregistered). Send £1 with the K7 form. There is no fee if the land is registered. For the reasons explained above the position in Scotland is different. It may be that an Inhibition (ie, blocking order) can be placed on the sale of the home pending settlement of a matrimonial property claim. Advice should be sought from a solicitor.

If your divorce is completed before the court has decided the long-term division of the property, your solicitor should seek permission from the court to re-register the charge to protect your right of occupation and interest in the property until a settlement is reached.

If you are not married

If you both own your home, you have equal rights to live there until the court decides on long-term ownership. Neither of you can borrow more money on a mortgage or sell the home without the other's signature (see pages 78 and 107 if you are pressured or misled into signing a mortgage). However, if you have dependent children you can apply for a property transfer order for their benefit (see page 113).

If your home is in your partner's sole name and you do not own a share, you are entitled to occupy it only if you have his permission. If you are asked to leave, your right to live there will end. However, it may be possible to get an injunction to exclude your partner if he has been violent (see page 104). In addition, you can try to establish that you *do* own a share in the home (for example, if you paid the deposit, paid for building works or, perhaps, carried them out yourself, or contributed towards the mortgage payments – see page 114). You should register a 'pending action' once you start court proceedings. This should prevent the property being sold or mortgaged before the court makes its ruling. Where you should make the registration depends on whether the property is registered or unregistered (see page 108). If it is registered, send form 63 with the fee of £40; if it is unregistered, send form K3 and £1. If there are dependent children of your relationship, you can apply for a transfer of the property for their benefit (see page 113).

WHAT TO DO IN THE LONG TERM

You and your partner have to decide how to share your property and money. If you want to remain in your home, you must make this quite clear to your solicitor. You may be worried that you will not be able to afford to pay the mortgage(s), but most people can cut their costs or increase their income in some of the ways described in Chapters two to five. Check these carefully. You may have to convince your solicitor as well as yourself about the options available.

This section explains the legal guidelines which the court and your solicitor will be bearing in mind. It is important that you know about them.

You may also be worried that your home is in need of repair. At the time of any property transfer you should ask your lender for an additional loan to keep or put your home in good condition (see page 91). If you are on income support, you should get the extra interest paid (see pages 32 and 38). Check whether you may be entitled to a grant from your local authority (see Chapter seven).

If you are married

If you are separating you may be thinking about applying for a divorce or judicial separation. Before granting either of these, the judge has to be satisfied with the proposed arrangements for the children. S/he can also deal with applications for maintenance for either partner (usually not for children these days, see page 118) and applications relating to property. The general guidelines for assessing what you will receive are given in the Matrimonial Causes Act 1973 (as amended). The Scottish equivalent is the Family Law (Scotland) Act 1985. This Act says that first consideration will be given to the children of the marriage. The court has wide powers to take into account all the circumstances of the case including, for example, the income and needs of both partners and the contribution they have made to the welfare of the family.

In England and Wales if you do not want a divorce or judicial separation, you can still apply to the court to have your share of the property assessed under the Married Women's Property Act 1882.

How the court decides

As part of divorce or separation proceedings the court can order almost any arrangement it wishes, provided it thinks it is fair to both parties. It is therefore important that your solicitor asks for all you want. The court must consider whether it is appropriate to end the financial relationship between the two parties to a marriage, in other words, to help the parties make a 'clean break'. However, it has never been possible to make a 'clean break' from your financial responsibilities to your child. So, with the Child Support Act (see page 118), an 'absent parent' will have to maintain his children even if a 'clean break' order was made before the Act came in (although the government may be considering changing this). The power of the court to order a 'clean break' between spouses, even if one party does not agree, is given by the Matrimonial and Family Proceedings Act 1984 or the Family Law (Scotland) Act 1985.

There are no rigid rules to decide what share of the value of the home you should have, or what the level of maintenance should be (except *child* maintenance, see page 119). You do not have to accept the first offer that your solicitor recommends to you. It may be possible to negotiate, or to persuade the court to order a better arrangement. Only if one partner's conduct has been extremely bad will the court take it into account in deciding what order to make.

What type of orders can the court make?

In practice, in the majority of cases, agreements about what will happen to the home are negotiated between your solicitor and your husband's solicitor before the court hearing. If the court is satisfied the agreement is fair and caters for the needs of the children, it will make an order based on the agreement. If you and your husband cannot reach agreement about what will happen to the home, the court will have to make the decision as to what would be appropriate to order. It is best to try to reach agreement before the court hearing, as otherwise you are likely to be faced with a greater statutory charge under the legal aid scheme (see Appendix 6) when proceedings have been finalised.

Negotiating a settlement over the home is very important. Your future security and your children's is at stake. Remember it is you who are instructing your solicitor, and you should make it clear if you want to try and keep your home. Some solicitors may not be fully aware of the extent of welfare benefit provision (see Chapters two, three and four).

The court can order:

- ☐ **an outright sale:** the court can order the home to be sold and the proceeds divided between you and your husband in proportions which it considers fair. What is considered fair will depend on the needs and resources of each of you. This type of order is unlikely to be made where there are dependent children unless the court is satisfied they will continue to have a home. In Scotland, where the home is owned jointly, there may need to be an Action of Division and Sale;

- ☐ **the sale to be postponed:** in England and Wales this is often called a 'Mesher' order. The court may transfer the home to you, but order that it be sold when the youngest child is no longer dependent, or when you remarry or cohabit. At the time of sale, the proceeds are divided between you and your husband in proportions set out in the court order.

This type of order is commonly suggested by solicitors. However, it can have disadvantages at the time of sale. If you do not have the earning capacity or the borrowing ability to raise enough money to buy your husband's share or to buy somewhere else, you may be faced with homelessness. If your children are then no longer dependent on you, even if they still live with you, you may not have a 'priority need' and so may not be entitled to be given accommodation by your local authority (see page 138).

At the time the agreement over the home is being negotiated, try to establish with your solicitor what proportion your husband's share is likely to be, and seek advice on whether it may be possible for you to raise this now in order to prevent the possible loss of your home later (see below);

☐ **a lump sum to be paid to the outgoing partner:** with this type of order one partner simply buys the other out. The court order will set out your respective shares based on the needs and resources of each of you.

You might wish to consider negotiating for a larger share of the home by making concessions as to the level of maintenance for yourself you will accept. Maintenance is only useful if you actually receive it and, particularly if payments cannot be relied upon, it would be better to seek a greater proportion of the home in exchange. You should discuss this possibility with your solicitor. However, child support payments are not negotiable (see page 118) – although you do not have to apply for them unless you are on income support, family credit or disability working allowance.

Note that, if you are on income support (or have been during the last 26 weeks), or your husband was claiming it during the last 26 weeks while you were living together, you may well have difficulty getting the interest on a loan to buy out your husband paid by the Benefits Agency. This is something your solicitor should take into account in the negotiations. If you take over the *existing* mortgage liability, without increasing it, there should be no problem.

If you and your husband were not on income support – for example, because he was working – and you want to buy him out, you should, if at all possible, take out a loan *before* you claim income support. The lender will need some persuading that you will be able to make the payments. It is possible that the Benefits Agency may be willing to indicate that, if you meet the financial and other criteria for income support, you will get the interest paid if you subsequently make a claim for the benefit. It is very important that you get advice about this (see Appendix 7).

Never go to a finance company for a loan as you will be charged a very high rate of interest, and if you are unable to meet these payments, debts will build up very quickly;

☐ **an outright property transfer:** the property is wholly transferred to one partner. The court will generally only make this type of order where there are exceptional circumstances – for example, where one partner clearly has a much greater need for the home; where there has been extremely bad conduct by one partner; where one partner clearly has far greater resources than the other; or to facilitate a clean break where it would be fair to do so. This type of order may also be made where there is very little or no equity in the home to divide between the partners and one partner has a greater need for the home.

If you are already divorced

You may feel that you could have come to a more satisfactory arrangement at the time of your divorce if you had considered the alternatives more carefully.

However, apart from maintenance payments, it is not possible to vary the original court order unless there are exceptional circumstances. You can, however, apply to vary a maintenance order for yourself if your circumstances or your ex-husband's circumstances change. Similarly, child support payments can be 'reviewed' by the Child Support Agency (see page 120). Where the court has made a 'clean break' order (see page 110), the court may say you cannot reapply for maintenance or it may order maintenance for a limited period, and say that you cannot come back to extend the period.

If you had no property settlement at the time of your divorce you can apply later, provided neither of you has remarried. If one of you has remarried, you can apply under the Married Women's Property Act 1882 to declare your interest in your property, but this must be done within three years of the decree absolute. You cannot apply in Scotland.

If you are not married

If you are not married, you have only limited protection and must rely on the general law of property. However, it is possible under s15 of the Children Act 1989 for the court to order the transfer of a property to a child or to an adult for the benefit of a child. By applying for this type of order it may be possible to secure long-term occupation of the home for you and your child(ren). You will need advice about this.

Where the home is jointly owned

If the home is jointly owned, you have a clear right to live there and share its value if it is sold. However, except where a transfer is necessary for the benefit of a child, the court cannot order that it is transferred into your name, unless there are very unusual circumstances (see page 113); it can only decide the proportion each party owns and order the sale or a postponed sale.

If you want to stay in your home, you can:

- ☐ try to raise the money to buy your partner out. See Chapters two, three and four for how to increase your income and Chapter five for how to lower your mortgage costs (but also see pages 38 and 112 about the difficulty in getting the costs paid if you are already on income support). Then ask your building society or local authority for a new mortgage;

- ☐ try to postpone the sale. You could try to argue that the sale of your home should be postponed if you have children and the property was intended as a home for them. The court has the power under Section 30 of the Law of Property Act 1925 to postpone the sale if 'any person interested' applies. In Scotland you would have to raise an action of aliment and seek to inhibit the sale;

- ☐ apply for a property transfer order for the benefit of the child(ren) under s15 of the Children Act 1989.

Where the home is solely owned by your partner

You have no automatic right to the home even if your relationship has lasted a long time and there are children. If the home is solely owned by your partner you can try, however, to:

- ☐ claim a share in the home. It can be difficult to establish that you are entitled to a share of the home unless it can be shown this was agreed at the outset. Recently, the courts have held that even where you can show you have directly contributed to the property, either by a deposit, making payments or improving the property, you also need to show that, in doing so, there was agreement, or it was intended, that this would entitle you to a share in the property. However, the courts are quite willing to assume that that must have been the intention if you have made significant payments. Looking after the home and children and paying the bills (even if this allowed your partner to pay the mortgage) will not by itself entitle you to a share of the home. If you think you are entitled to a share you can start proceedings under s30 of the Law of Property Act 1925. You will need legal advice on taking these proceedings and on claiming a share of the home;

- [ ] extend the time in which you can live in it even if you fail to establish a financial interest in your home. You will need to convince the court that the purpose of your partner, in setting up the home, was to provide for you and any children, and/or you gave up secure accommodation to go and live there. Sometimes, it may even be possible to ask the court to order the transfer of the property into your name, if this was the understanding between you at the time;
- [ ] apply for a transfer of property for the benefit of any children of your relationship under s15 of the Children Act 1989. (There is no equivalent Scottish provision but parents are liable to support their children, as in England and Wales.)

Note: whenever you take court proceedings relating to your home, you should immediately register a 'pending action'. This applies whether you are married or unmarried. Ask your solicitor for advice.

HOW TO NEGOTIATE WITH YOUR LENDER

So far, your legal rights to the home as against your partner's have been described. But if there is a mortgage on the home and you are hoping to keep on paying it yourself in the future, you will also need to negotiate with your lender to obtain their agreement to your plans. The attitude of your lender will probably vary depending on whether or not the mortgage is now in arrears.

If there are no mortgage arrears

If you have no arrears and want to try to make the payments in future you must write to your lender and explain the position. Ask them to agree to make any arrangements which would help you financially as described in chapter two, and to give you time to make them. If you are hoping that ownership of the home will be transferred to you as part of a divorce or property settlement, explain that to your lender.

Problems

Sometimes people find that lenders will not accept mortgage payments from them. Even if your lender will not accept you as the borrower, pay the instalments and keep a record of your payments. This will be important if you need to show the court that you are acting in good faith. As well as sending payments, you should point out any legal rights under family or property law that you have or are claiming. These will depend on whose name the home is now in and whose name is on the mortgage deed:

- ☐ If the home and mortgage deed are **in your name or joint names**: as owner, you are entitled to make the payments.

- ☐ If the home and mortgage deed are **in your spouse's name**: you are entitled under section 1(5) of the Matrimonial Homes Act 1983 to make the payments in their place, and you should draw your lender's attention to this Act. The equivalent power is contained in the Matrimonial Homes (Family Protection) (Scotland) Act 1981 s2(1).

- ☐ If the home and mortgage deed are in **your partner's name and you are not married**: you are not liable to make payments and your lender is not obliged to accept them. However, you may wish to make payments in order to stay in the home and while you are trying to pursue rights to the home (see pages 109 and 114). Ask your lender to accept payments while you are doing this.

If the mortgage is in arrears now

If the mortgage is in arrears now, the lender may already have started taking action against you or your partner or against you both. The action the lender will take, and what you can do to stop the action, is explained in Chapter six. Ask for a statement of recent payments and notify the lender if you are on income support or will be applying for it. Whatever stage the proceedings have reached, you may still be able to keep your home. You can try to clear the mortgage arrears (see Chapter six). You may be able to backdate an income support claim if your partner has stopped making payments (see page 47). If you are divorcing, you should ask your lender to postpone any further action until after the court has decided on the property settlement. Start to pay the mortgage instalments as soon as you find out there are arrears. If you cannot afford the whole monthly payment to start with, send as much as you can with a letter explaining your situation. You should get advice from a solicitor about your position straightaway, especially if the mortgage is in your partner's sole name.

INCOME AFTER SEPARATION

So far, this chapter has concentrated on your rights to stay in the home after you and your partner separate. You will also need to consider what financial help you are entitled to for day-to-day living expenses. This section deals with this. It is sensible to get advice from a solicitor as soon as possible (see Appendix 6 about how to find a suitable one).

In this section, we look at things mainly from the point of view of the woman and assume that she has care of the children. However, the rules apply in the same way to men as they do to women.

It will clearly be very important that you get as much income as possible for yourself and any children who live with you. You may be able to reach agreement with your ex-partner about how much he should pay you or, if you are married, you can apply to the court for a maintenance order for yourself. In divorce or judicial separation proceedings, you can also ask for payment of a lump sum or a transfer of property order – for example, an order that the house should be transferred to you (see page 112). You cannot ask for these orders if you are not married, except very rarely (see page 114). As far as children you look after are concerned, you now generally have to apply to the Child Support Agency for a maintenance assessment.

Duty to maintain you if you are on income support

If you are receiving income support and have separated from your husband but are not divorced, he is 'liable to maintain' you. He can be taken to a magistrates' court by the Benefits Agency if he fails to do so. This can include being prosecuted. The Benefits Agency can recover from him the income support they pay you. The court can, however, order him to pay more than this – any excess is then paid to you.

There is no set amount that has to be paid. If you cannot reach agreement between yourselves, it may be possible for your husband to reach agreement with the Benefits Agency.

His liability to pay ceases on divorce as far as the Benefits Agency is concerned (but, of course, you can ask for the orders referred to above in divorce proceedings). Parents also have a liability to maintain their children, and this liability does survive divorce. In practice, however, the Child Support Act will now normally be used for child maintenance (see below).

Welfare benefits for separated partners

Immediately you separate, you should consider whether you might be entitled to any social security benefits. It makes no difference whether you are married or not. If you are working 16 hours a week or more, see Chapter two. If you work less than 16 hours a week or you do no paid work, see Chapter three. Council tax benefit is explained in Chapter four. Note that, for income support, you may be entitled to benefit in your own right even if you are still living in the same house as your ex-partner, if Benefits Agency staff accept that you are living separate lives.

Whether you are working or not, if you are raising dependent children, consider claiming one parent benefit. This is an addition to child benefit and is worth £6.15 a week (1994/95 rates). However, one parent benefit is taken into account in full if you are getting income support, and will therefore only be of benefit if it is sufficient to lift you off income support altogether. Even in that event, however, you should bear in mind that you will then lose entitlement to things like free school meals (see page 48) and most social fund payments (see pages 49-51). Usually, you cannot get one parent benefit until you have been separated for 13 weeks.

If you are on income support and you get child benefit for a child living with you, you are entitled to a lone parent premium as part of your income support. This is worth £5.10 a week for 1994/95. In addition, £15 of your net, part-time earnings will be ignored when working out your income support.

Maintenance for children living with you: the Child Support Act

Does the Act apply to you?

Under the Child Support Act, anyone with care of a child under 16 (or 19 if s/he is in full-time, secondary education) can apply to the Child Support Agency (CSA) for a 'maintenance assessment' against a parent not living with the child (called an 'absent parent'). Not only *parents* with care' can apply – anyone with day-to-day care can. Usually, of course, it will be a parent.

However, if there was a court order or a maintenance agreement relating to child maintenance in force before April 1993 (when the Act came in), and you as the parent with care are *not* on income support, family credit or disability working allowance, you cannot apply for an assessment until some time between April 1996 and April 1997 (exactly when depends on your surname).

If you are a parent with care and *are* getting one of those benefits, the CSA will require you to apply for a maintenance assessment (note that this only applies to *parents* with care). This is even if there was already a court order or maintenance agreement in force before April 1993. However, you do not have to apply if the CSA accepts that there would be a risk of 'harm or undue distress' to you or any children living with you if you had to make an application. 'Harm or undue distress' is not defined in the rules. It would certainly include things such as violence but is in fact much broader than this. It is very important that you get advice before agreeing to apply for a maintenance assessment if you are not sure that you want your ex-partner to pay maintenance (see Appendix 7). You may prefer to take the benefit penalty, if you can afford to (see below).

Benefit penalty

If you cannot show 'harm or undue distress' but still decline to cooperate, a benefit penalty ('reduced benefit direction') will be given. This means that (at 1994/95 rates) £9.14 will be deducted from your benefit for six months and £4.57 for a further 12 months (unless, in the meantime, you do cooperate or fall outside the scheme, for example because the child ceases to live with you). Before finally deciding to impose a penalty, however, the child support officer must consider the welfare of any children who might be affected by it.

How much will you get?

As part of the assessment procedure, both the person with care and the absent parent have to provide detailed information about their financial circumstances and so on. If the absent parent does not cooperate the CSA can issue an **interim maintenance assessment** requiring him to pay more than he would otherwise have to. Again, however, the child support officer must consider the welfare of any children who might be affected.

There is a complicated formula for working out how much the absent parent will have to pay. It is based on the notional cost of bringing up the child and the absent parent's circumstances, such as his income and housing costs, as well as the person with care's income. The CSA must apply the formula rigidly – it has no discretion to adapt it in particular situations. For further information, see CPAG's *Child Support Handbook* (see Appendix 9).

The minimum amount payable is £2.30 per week. Even absent parents on income support generally have to pay this amount. There are some exceptions – for example, if the absent parent is under 18 or receives an incapacity or disability benefit in addition to income support. If the exceptions do not apply, deductions can be made from the absent parent's benefit (unless certain other deductions are already being made). In addition, some absent parents not on income support do not have to pay any maintenance – for example, if an absent parent receives an incapacity or disability benefit, or has any child living with him for at least part of the week, and in either case the amount assessed under the formula is £2.30 or less a week.

How will you be paid?

As the person with care, you can ask for the maintenance to be paid to the CSA rather than to you. This is useful if you think that payments are likely to be irregular or you do not want the absent parent to know where you live. If you are on income support, you then get the same amount of money even if a payment is missed. If a payment is missed, the CSA will then chase it automatically. If payments are, instead, due to be made to you but are not, you can ask the CSA to chase the absent parent.

The CSA has a number of powers to enforce payment. These include requiring an employer to make deductions from the absent parent's wages.

Reviews and challenging a decision

Child support assessments are reviewed automatically every 12 months. In addition, a person with care or absent parent can apply for a review at any time if there has been a significant change of circumstances – in other words, one which will make a difference of at least £10 per week (or sometimes £1 or £5 a week) to the amount of child maintenance which has to be paid.

It is also possible to challenge most child support officer decisions by asking for a review, and then appealing to a Child Support Appeal Tribunal if you are still unhappy. A parent with care can also appeal a benefit penalty (see page 119) to a tribunal (without having to ask for a review first). Most review requests or appeals have to be put in within 28 days, so it is important that you get advice from one of the organisations listed in Appendix 7 as soon as possible.

How maintenance and other payments are dealt with if you are on benefit

If you are getting **income support**, payments which are made, or are due to be made, to you at regular intervals by a 'liable relative' (see below) normally count as part of your income. That will affect the amount of income support which you get and may disqualify you altogether. Occasionally such payments are counted as capital. On the other hand, lump sums are sometimes treated as income (but not if they result from the disposal of a house or other form of capital because of separation, or divorce or judicial separation proceedings). The rules are, in fact, quite complicated. See CPAG's *National Welfare Benefits Handbook* (Appendix 9) for further details. The term **'liable relative'** includes a former spouse (even though former spouses are not 'liable to maintain' in the sense explained on page 117).

Child support payments are counted in full if you are on income support.

If you are getting **family credit** or **disability working allowance**, the first £15 per week of maintenance payments is ignored in working out your income. This includes child support payments.

What matters, in most cases, is the actual payments made, not how much is due. With child support payments, however, if the recent average is more than was due under the assessment, you take the latter figure.

INCOME TAX FOR SEPARATED PARTNERS

Although your tax position may change on separation, your tax code will not be altered unless you let your tax office know what has happened. You should do this straightaway and, when writing, ask the tax office to send you leaflet IR92, *Income Tax – A Guide for One Parent Families*, if you have children. As it is the woman left in the home who has most problems with tax, it is her situation that is discussed in the main in this section. The current levels of tax allowances are set out at the end of this chapter. The situation will depend on whether you are married or living together.

- ☐ **Unmarried partners:** the tax system takes no account of people who live together as husband and wife but who are not legally married. Therefore, if you and your partner separate and you are not married to one another that will not, by itself, affect your tax position. In this section, we therefore concentrate mainly on married couples.

- ☐ **Married partners:** before 6 April 1993, the married couple's allowance normally went to the husband. Since that date, it has been possible for spouses living together to agree that it should go to the wife instead, or you can split it equally between you (see leaflet IR80, *Income Tax and Married Couples*, available from any tax office). In the year of separation, each of you will continue to get the amount of the allowance you were getting at the time you separated.

Note that the nature of this allowance changed in April 1994. It is no longer an amount of income you receive without paying the tax. Instead, it operates as a tax relief (at 20 per cent in 1994/95, 15 per cent in 1995/96), reducing your tax bill in that way. In 1994/95, the allowance is £1,720, so the tax saving is 20 per cent of that which comes to £344.

The additional personal allowance

You can claim the additional personal allowance if you are bringing up a child on your own. The child must be living with you. S/he must be under 16 or in full-time education, or training full-time for at least two years for a trade or profession (for example, a youth training programme). If the child lives with someone else for part of the year, the allowance is divided between you (you can agree on the proportion, or the Inland Revenue will decide). Only one allowance is payable, no matter how many children live with you.

This allowance brings your own personal allowance up to the same amount as the married couple's allowance. So, if you are already getting half that allowance, you can claim additional personal allowance to bring you up to the amount of the full married couple's allowance. You can claim the additional personal allowance against your income for the full year in which you and your husband separate and for each subsequent year, unless you remarry.

Mortgage interest relief

Most people no longer need to *claim* mortgage interest relief, because they receive it automatically in the form of reduced repayments to the lender. This arrangement is called MIRAS and is explained on page 12. You will only need to apply for tax relief on the mortgage if it is outside the MIRAS scheme. In order to qualify for relief – whether under MIRAS or by claiming it – you have to be paying interest on a loan to buy your home. You can get relief on a loan up to £30,000 at 20 per cent (15 per cent in 1995/96). Note that, unlike housing costs with income support (see page 32), you cannot get relief for loans for home improvements or repairs.

If you separate, the amount of relief available to you will depend on what arrangements you make for the payment of interest. If you pay the interest or your ex-partner gives you money to pay the interest, you will get relief. You will also get it if he makes payments on your behalf to the lender. Note that, since the introduction of separate taxation in April 1990, it has been possible for *married* couples to have their mortgage tax relief divided between them in any proportion they want. If you and your husband have separated you may want to write to the tax office and cancel any earlier 'allocation of interest election' (as it is called). You will need advice about this (see Appendix 7).

If both of you are buying homes, you can each get relief. As a general rule, you only get mortgage interest relief on one house at a time. However, if you move away from your old home but cannot sell it, you can get relief on two homes, of up to £30,000 in each case, for up to 12 months (or up to three years if you have particular difficulty selling). This could apply even though your ex-partner remains in the old home while you try to sell it.

Note also that you can get tax relief to buy a *larger* share in the home. So, if you borrow money to buy out your former partner, you will get relief on that loan (up to a total of £30,000). Similarly, you may be able to get income support housing costs for such a purpose but see page 38.

See, generally, leaflets IR123, *Mortgage Interest Relief*, and IR93, *Separation, Divorce and Maintenance Payments*, available from any tax office.

Maintenance

As a separated spouse, you will need to sort out what maintenance payments are due to you, and how they will be paid.

- [ ] **Is the payment voluntary?** If your husband pays you maintenance as a result of an informal agreement, that money is completely disregarded for tax purposes. He cannot claim tax relief on what he pays you, and you will not be taxed on what you receive. The same applies to payments made by someone to whom you were not married.

- [ ] **Is the payment made to you under a court order or written maintenance agreement?** Following the Finance Act 1988, the rules about taxation of maintenance payments differ depending on the date of the court order or the written maintenance agreement. The 'new rules' apply to the following arrangements:

    – all new court orders applied for on or after 15 March 1988;

    – all new court orders made after 30 June 1988;

    – written maintenance agreements made on or after 15 March 1988 (except those relating to an old court order or agreement);

    – payments due on or after 15 March 1988 under agreements made before that date which were not received by the tax office by 30 June 1988;

    – maintenance assessments made by the Child Support Agency on or after 6 April 1993 (except assessments which replace agreements and orders made before 15 March 1988).

    The 'old rules' apply to the following:

    – court orders made before 15 March 1988;

    – court orders made by 30 June 1988 which were applied for on or before 15 March 1988;

    – maintenance agreements made before 15 March 1988;

    – the two exceptions listed under the 'new rules' above.

For details of the new and old rules see below.

The new rules

Tax position of payer
If you are or were married, and have been ordered or agreed to pay maintenance, you should pay it without deducting any tax. You will receive tax relief on the payments up to the amount of the married couple's allowance (£1,720 in 1994/95). You will not get tax relief on payments over this amount. Tax relief is given by way of an adjustment to your PAYE code.

Note that the relief is, in 1994/95, given at only 20 per cent, and in 1995/96 will be at 15 per cent.

To qualify for relief, the payments must be for the maintenance of the spouse or ex-spouse, or for the maintenance of a child under 21 of whom you are both parents (or whom you have treated as part of your family). Child support payments (see page 118) qualify. Note that no relief is available for payments made *to* a child; they must be made to someone *for* the child.

Relief is available for any bills you pay on your spouse's behalf, such as mortgage capital, as long as you are required to do so by a court order or written agreement.

If your spouse remarries you will cease getting tax relief on maintenance you pay.

If you were not married to your partner, you will not be able to claim tax relief for maintenance for you or the children (including child support payments).

Tax position of recipient

If you are or were married, you do not pay tax on any form of maintenance payments received from your husband, even if you remarry. Nor do you pay tax **if you were not married.**

The old rules

Tax position of payer

If you are or were married, you can get tax relief on payments paid to your spouse but only up to the amount of relief you were getting in 1988/89. You should pay the sums 'gross' – ie, without deducting any tax. There are special rules for payments to children (including children over 21). If you pay maintenance, it is possible to switch to the new rules. You may wish to do this if and when the amount of the married couple's allowance exceeds the payments on which you got tax relief in 1988/89. Note that you cannot then switch back. You should write to your spouse within 30 days of the switch so that she knows that she need not pay tax on future payments (see below).

Unmarried partners cannot get relief.

Tax position of recipient

If you are or were married, you pay tax on payments received from your spouse, but the first £1,720 (at 1994/95 rates) is exempt, unless you remarry. Also, if the payments increase, the amount on which you pay tax cannot be more than the amount on which you paid tax in 1988/89. If you receive payments from a partner to whom you were **not married,** you do not get the £1,720 exemption.

If your maintenance fluctuates, you may end up paying tax under the old rules on money you have yet to receive. You can prevent this happening in the future by having your wages and your maintenance for the current year taxed separately. Ask the tax office to set all your personal allowances against your pay from work and, at the same time, ask for your maintenance to be taxed 'under schedule D'. You will then pay tax on your wages in the normal way. Halfway through the tax year, you will get a tax bill relating to your maintenance for that year. You can ask for payment to be deferred until the end of the tax year when you are certain how much maintenance you have received in the course of the year. At the end of the year, you can then ask to pay the tax bill in instalments, rather than as a lump sum, to relieve hardship. One suggestion is to ask to pay the tax for the previous year through the PAYE system. Remember, maintenance received under the new rules is not taxable, so this problem does not arise.

See, generally, leaflets IR92, *A Guide for One-Parent Families*, and IR93, *Separation, Divorce and Maintenance Payments*, available from any tax office.

Other problems

- ☐ **Backdated claims:** you may have realised that you have not claimed all the allowances you could have since you separated. Do not panic. You can ask for a reassessment of the tax you have paid during the last six years.

- ☐ **Inaccessible tax office:** you may need to discuss your case with a tax inspector, but find that your tax matters are dealt with by an office at the other end of the country. You can ask for your papers to be sent to an office in your area and arrange a personal interview with an inspector there.

- ☐ **If you stop work:** you may need to stop work and stay at home to look after your children. See Chapter three for details about income support. You should let your tax office know and claim a tax rebate (because the tax you have been paying will have been assessed on the assumption that you would work for the whole year). Make a claim immediately. If you wait until the end of the tax year before making your claim, the process of checking and sending your rebate will be much longer. If you stop work and are unemployed, that is, you are 'signing on' at the unemployment benefit office, you will not be able to claim your tax rebate until you start working again or until the end of the tax year, whichever comes first.

The main tax allowances for tax year April 1994/95

	£
Personal allowance (up to age 64)	3,445
Married couple's allowance (up to age 64)	1,720
Additional personal allowance for looking after children	1,720

Note: for the tax year 1994/95 the rates of tax paid on income (after deducting tax allowances) are:

20 per cent on £0-£3,000
25 per cent on £3,001-23,700
40 per cent on over £23,700

CHAPTER NINE

If you lose your home

If your lender obtains possession of your home, you will need to ensure that your house is sold quickly for a price which clears your debt, or minimises the amount outstanding, and that you are able to find somewhere else to live.

This chapter examines what happens to your house after it is repossessed and what options you have if there is negative equity (ie, you owe more than the house is worth). It also explains where you can look for new accommodation, and what rights you have to be rehoused by the local authority.

It can be difficult to find alternative accommodation so never agree to the sale of your home until you definitely have somewhere else to live. If you are moving because you and your partner are separating, read Chapter eight carefully to see how you should ask for the proceeds from the sale of your present home to be split.

It is important that you contact your local authority as soon as possible. They may only be able to register your name on the housing waiting list, but they may also have an advice centre which can help you with your mortgage difficulties. Contact the local authority immediately if you think you may become homeless.

IF YOUR HOME IS REPOSSESSED

If your lender is granted a possession order (in Scotland, the equivalent is an ejection order) and you have been evicted by the bailiffs (in Scotland, Sheriff's Officers), the lender will sell your home, take what is owed from the proceeds, deduct legal and estate agent's fees, repay any other lenders usually in the order in which they registered their charges, and give you what is left over.

It is a good idea to ask the court to allow you time to sell your home yourself, even though they have granted possession to the lender because, if you were to sell on the open market, you might be able to get a higher price for your home than your lender would. If it is apparent that you are not going to be able to clear the arrears and it is inevitable that the lender is going to get an outright possession order at court, you should discuss the position with the local authority's housing department if you are intending to sell the house yourself. Some local authorities take the view that if you sell the home voluntarily you will have become homeless intentionally (see page 138). If you seek their views in advance of the sale it makes it more difficult for them to say this. If they do suggest that you would be making yourself intentionally homeless, you should seek advice from one of the organisations listed in Appendix 7 about challenging this position.

When selling the house or flat, after you have been evicted, the lender is legally obliged to try to get the best price reasonably obtainable at the time. The lender will be advised by estate agents what the sale price should be. Unfortunately, particularly in a depressed property market, it can take many months for the house or flat to be sold. You should remember that, simply because the lender has evicted you, this does not mean that interest stops building up on the loan.

Interest will continue to build up until the house is sold. The same applies if you hand in the keys to the property voluntarily to the lender before court action (if you do this the local authority may also consider you are intentionally homeless, but see page 139). If there is a delay in the property being sold it may be possible to agree with the lender to the sale price being dropped below what the estate agents consider is the market value to enable the property to be sold quickly. However, this will not be possible if there are lenders who have second or subsequent charges who will not be paid off if the property is sold at less than the market value.

If you think that your lender is being unreasonable in refusing to agree to a sale, and you can demonstrate that you will suffer financially as a result, you may be able to apply to the court for an order forcing a sale under the 1925 Law of Property Act. If you think this is the case, you should obtain legal advice urgently.

If building societies sell following eviction, they are obliged to send you details of the date of the sale, the sale price and the name of the purchaser. If there is any money left over after the mortgage (or mortgages if there are more than one) has been paid off, it will be sent to you. If this is likely to be the case then you should make sure that the lender knows where you live. However, if there is likely to be no surplus then you may not need to tell the lender where you are living.

IF THE SALE PRICE DOES NOT CLEAR THE DEBTS

If the property is sold and its sale price is insufficient to clear all the debts, some lenders may simply write off the outstanding debt if it is not a large amount or claim the shortfall from the indemnity insurance.

Indemnity insurance is paid for by the borrower when the loan is first taken out. Most mortgage lenders insist on this insurance if the loan is more than 70-80 per cent of the value of the property.

Although paid for by the borrower, the insurance protects the lender against a loss from the proceeds of sale. If a lender claims on the indemnity insurance, the insurance company can pursue the borrower for the amount of the loss. Some larger insurers say they will not pursue these debts in cases of genuine hardship. However, an increasing number of borrowers are faced with substantial demands from insurers following a claim by their lender.

If you are faced with demands for repayment of outstanding debts after the sale of your house, from either your lender or their insurers, there are at least two possible solutions you can negotiate.

- ☐ If you have no money at all to offer them and are likely to remain in this position for some time, you should ask them to write off the debt. Some borrowers, especially those who can show that they have made every effort to minimise the loss, have been successful in doing this.

- ☐ If you are able to raise a sum smaller than that which is outstanding you can offer this in 'full and final settlement' of the debt. However, it is important to ensure that the money is being accepted on this basis by the lender. You should seek expert advice before making such an offer.

You should ask the lender for a detailed breakdown of the debt which they claim you owe. It will probably contain a large number of fees, for instance, for administration, solicitors' and estate agents' services. If any of these appear unreasonable, you should challenge them.

You should check if the lenders have claimed against their indemnity policy. If not, you should ask to see a copy of the policy and have an explanation of their reason for their not claiming.

If you have separated from your joint owner you should ensure that the lender is pursuing them for payment as well, otherwise you may find yourself having to pay for the full shortfall.

You could also consider if the shortfall has arisen because the valuation on which your mortgage was based was too high. If this is the case the lender may have a legal claim against the surveyors or solicitors who acted on their behalf at the time of the sale. If they have not mitigated their loss by pursuing this claim, they will find it more difficult to enforce your debt to them in the courts. If you are unable to negotiate successfully with your lender and the sums owed are very large, it might be worth considering discharging your debt by petitioning for bankruptcy. However, becoming bankrupt is an expensive process and will make it almost impossible to obtain any credit until your bankruptcy is discharged. You may also lose any remaining assets you have, and bankruptcy carries a social stigma which may effect your employment and other prospects. But carrying the burden of a massive debt (the average negative equity on property repossessed in 1992 was estimated at over £20,000) for the rest of your life might outweigh these problems.

If you are in this position, seek help from a Citizens Advice Bureau or Money Advice Centre (see Appendix 7).

If your partner is declared bankrupt, you should get legal advice to establish the rights you have to the home as against those of your partner's creditors. Even though you may be living in the house, it is possible for your partner's trustee in bankruptcy to apply to court for an order to evict you and any children to enable the property to be sold with vacant possession to pay off your partner's creditors. The Insolvency Act 1986 (in Scotland, the Bankruptcy (Scotland) Act 1985) permits a bankrupt's spouse and children to remain as occupiers for one year but only in very exceptional circumstances will eviction be delayed beyond this period. You should get legal advice straightaway.

MORTGAGE RESCUE SCHEMES

A number of building societies are setting up mortgage rescue schemes as an alternative to seeking possession. The schemes are being developed with housing associations who will purchase the property and allow borrowers to remain in their homes as either tenants or on a shared ownership basis (see page 7).

The *Council of Mortgage Lenders Arrears Management Manual* suggests that mortgage rescue schemes can help borrowers who meet all of the following criteria.

- ☐ No other assistance is more appropriate to their circumstances.

- ☐ They are not receiving income support to meet their mortgage interest. Where this is paid direct they will be in no danger of losing their home.

- ☐ They have suffered a severe loss of income – for example, because of loss of earnings or relationship breakdown.

- ☐ They wish to remain in their property as tenants.

- ☐ They are able to afford the rent which the housing association will charge. Housing associations will therefore wish to know what liability borrowers have in respect of their previous mortgage and other debts.
- ☐ It is appropriate for the housing association to house them in the property in which they are living. Housing associations do not house people with high incomes, or who own large or luxurious properties. The property will also need to be in a reasonable state of repair.

Although there has been much publicity about mortgage rescue schemes they have been very slow to get off the ground. Many lenders do not operate the schemes and those that do may only do so in certain areas. A handful of local authorities have also tried to establish mortgage rescue schemes to prevent borrowers with priority need (see page 138) from becoming homeless.

You should ask your lender and your local authority whether they may be able to help you through a mortgage rescue scheme.

BUYING ANOTHER HOME

If you have enough cash from the sale of your former home, it may be possible for you to buy again. However, if you have had difficulties in paying for your present home, you must make sure that you do not have the same problems again. Consider buying a smaller, cheaper property (but not one in a poor state of repair), so that you will need a smaller mortgage. You could also consider a shared ownership scheme (see page 7).

Some building societies offer lower interest rate mortgages which are cheaper than conventional repayments mortgages (see page 3). These mortgages are generally only available to first-time buyers. If your previous mortgage was in your partner's name you would probably be classed as a first-time buyer; even if your previous mortgage was in your joint names, you may still be eligible.

Can you afford to buy again?

To decide whether or not you can buy again, you will need to find out how much a suitable home will cost and how much you can afford to pay.

How much can you pay?

The amount you can pay depends on the amount of capital you have and on the amount you can borrow on a mortgage.

☐ **How much capital can you raise?** Calculate how much you will have left over after the sale of your present home. You will first need to find out the value of your present home by asking two or three local estate agents what price you could hope to get. You will then have to find out the amount that you still owe, by asking your lenders for redemption figures (see page 69); working out the cost of selling (by getting estimates of the fees which will be charged by your estate agent, solicitor and removal firm); and working out the cost of buying again – by asking the solicitor for an estimate of the fee and putting aside a bit extra in case you have to pay for repairs to your new home. Deduct these costs from the value of your home to see how much capital you can rely on having left over.

If you are claiming social security benefits, any capital you have left over after the sale of your present home will be ignored by the Benefits Agency for up to six months from the date of sale. This period can be extended at the discretion of the Benefits Agency. This is the case as long as you are going to use the money to buy another home.
Note: If you are divorcing and have had legal aid to help with court costs, you may have to pay back some of the capital to the Legal Aid Board, see Appendix 6.

☐ **How much can you borrow on a mortgage?** This will depend on your income. You will have to give all the lenders who might grant you a mortgage the figures for your gross annual income and that of your partner. Ask them how much they are prepared to lend in principle. If you are not working, it is still possible to raise a mortgage even if you are receiving income support. You should ask staff at your local Benefits Agency if they will meet the interest payments on the loan you need. If they agree to this in principle, you can go back to your original lender, or find a new lender and ask if they will grant you a new loan (see page 68). But remember that income support will only cover the interest payments, not the capital or any endowment premium. For ways to try to meet these costs, see page 44. For the first 16 weeks on benefit, only 50 per cent of the interest will be met by your income support (see page 40) and the Benefits Agency can restrict any interest payments they think are excessive (see page 42). Also see page 37 if you are increasing your housing costs.

If you are selling your present home because you have fallen behind with your mortgage payments and have been unable to clear the arrears, you may well find it difficult to persuade your lender to grant you another mortgage. You will, however, be able to make a good case for getting another mortgage if you can show that the reason for the arrears will not occur again – for example, the cause of the arrears was the breakdown of your marriage or an illness from which you have now recovered. If this is not possible, you will probably have to pay cash or you will not be able to buy again.

How much will a suitable home cost?

Now that you know how much you can pay, find out if there is any chance of your getting a suitable home by looking in local newspapers and by contacting local estate agents. Although flats may appear cheaper than houses, it is worth remembering that you will probably have to pay a share of repair costs. Be very wary of blocks of flats with high service charges. For more about service charges and repairs if you own a flat, see Chapter seven.

How to raise a mortgage

If you will not have enough capital from the sale of your home to buy another home outright, you will have to consider how you can raise a mortgage.

From whom can you borrow?

The different types of lenders are described on pages 10-12. The cheapest arrangements are offered by building societies and banks, so you should only consider approaching them. Building societies are the most common source of money for people who are buying a home for the second time. If your previous lender was a building society, or if you have savings in a building society, contact that one first.

Many banks grant mortgages but they, like building societies, are likely to be wary of someone who has had difficulties making their mortgage payments in the past.

If you have tried these options and been refused, you can ask an estate agent, solicitor, bank manager or mortgage broker to refer you formally to a building society. Be very careful to check whether you will be charged a fee for this introduction and make sure that you are not obliged to take a very expensive form of mortgage. If a broker fails to get you a suitable mortgage, they are only allowed to charge £1 (Consumer Credit Act 1974). Brokers can, however, charge for any surveys and other work carried out on your behalf.

What type of mortgage should you get?

The different types of mortgages and possible government help with your payments are described in Chapter one. Briefly, if you want the lowest possible monthly payments you should try to obtain a capital repayment mortgage from a building society, bank or local authority.

How to apply for your mortgage if you are working

Write to the lender you have decided to approach first, stating:

- ☐ that you would like a capital repayment mortgage, and in whose name(s) it should be;
- ☐ your gross income and that of your partner (if any) and how this is made up. Give details of your basic pay, your regular overtime and bonuses, and any pay-rise you are to receive in the near future;
- ☐ the amount of capital you can put towards the purchase price;
- ☐ that you have calculated that you will be able to meet the mortgage payments (see Appendix 1) as well as your other commitments. Show that you have considered such costs as travelling to work and child-minding;
- ☐ why your circumstances led to your selling your last home and why any difficulties you had then will not recur. If you are asking someone other than your previous lender for this mortgage, you will have to explain why your previous lender was not willing to help you.

How to apply for your mortgage if you are receiving income support

First, write to the manager of the Benefits Agency office in the areas where you are hoping to buy, stating:

- ☐ that you are receiving income support. Give the address of your present office and your benefit reference number;
- ☐ that you have to leave your present home and are hoping to buy again to avoid becoming homeless;
- ☐ that you would like a letter confirming that the manager will, in principle, be prepared to include in your benefit the interest payments on any mortgage you raise within a reasonable limit. Say that you need this letter so you can show your lender how the mortgage interest payments will be made.

Then write to the lender you have decided to approach stating:

- ☐ that you would like a capital repayment mortgage;
- ☐ that you are enclosing a copy of the letter you have received from the Benefits Agency to show how the mortgage interest payments will be made;

- [ ] that, once you have found a suitable property and know the exact amount of the mortgage you will need, you will get a further letter from the Benefits Agency agreeing to meet the whole or part of the interest payments on that amount;

- [ ] that either you will meet the capital repayments and explain how you will do this (see page 44 for advice on this), or that you would like the lender to waive the capital part of the mortgage until you are in a position to start making payments towards the capital. Explain how and when this might be;

- [ ] the amount of capital you can put towards the purchase price;

- [ ] why your circumstances led to the sale of your last home and why any difficulties you had before will not recur.

If you are asking someone other than your previous lender for a mortgage, you will have to explain why your previous lender would not help.

Finally, when you have found the home you want to buy, write to the Benefits Agency again, stating the size of mortgage you need. Ask for a letter confirming that they will revise your weekly benefit to cover the interest payments on this amount. If you are increasing your mortgage costs, see page 37.

How to get a guarantor for your mortgage

As a condition of granting the mortgage your lender may insist that you provide a guarantor. A guarantor is someone who agrees to make the mortgage payments if you should fail to do so. If you are unable to provide a guarantor you may find your lender will not press for one; especially if other negotiations are going smoothly.

You can ask either an individual or the local authority to act as a guarantor for you. For a person to be acceptable to a lender they must have assets greater in value than your mortgage – for example, their own home – or have enough income after paying their own rent/mortgage to be able to pay yours if necessary.

Local authorities have powers under two different Acts to stand as guarantor:

- [ ] they can guarantee your mortgage payments and any extension of them under Section 442 of the Housing Act 1985; *or*

- [ ] the social services department may be able to guarantee your mortgage payments if you have children under s17 of the Children Act 1989. They are only likely to consider this if it will prevent your family from becoming homeless.

Appeals

If you feel your lender's insistence on a guarantor is unreasonable because you have shown how you can meet the mortgage repayments, or if your building society or local authority is not being very helpful, it may be possible to appeal against their decision (see page 71).

SHARED OWNERSHIP SCHEMES

You might be able to take part in a shared ownership scheme run by a housing association or local authority by using the capital from the sale of your house to purchase a share in another property with a view to buying it outright over a period paying by instalments. You should contact the Housing Corporation to see if there are any such schemes being run in your area (for the address, see Appendix 7). You may be entitled to claim housing benefit to cover the rent element of your housing costs (see page 24).

RENTED ACCOMMODATION

If you cannot raise a mortgage, there may be other ways of finding accommodation for your family. These are described very briefly below.

Private rented accommodation

This is always difficult to find, especially if you have children, and it is very often furnished which will mean little or no storage space for any furnishings you may have already acquired. Unfurnished, privately-rented accommodation is scarce. Local shop windows, newspapers and accommodation agencies are the main sources of information. However, always get advice before signing any agreements or paying any fees. You will probably need to have money for returnable deposits and rent in advance. You may also have to find money for premiums ('key money'). If you are on income support you may be able to claim money for rent in advance from the social fund. However, the money will be in the form of a loan and you will have to pay it back from your weekly benefit. See page 49 for details of the social fund.

Under Section 17 of the Children Act 1989 local authorities have a duty to 'safeguard and promote the welfare' of 'children in need' and to enable them to live with their families. If you have children who would otherwise be homeless, and therefore 'in need', you can ask your local authority's social services department to use its powers under this Act to pay a deposit or rent in advance so your children have somewhere to live. If you believe that you are entitled to this help and cannot get it, seek advice from one of the organisations listed in Appendix 7.

Housing associations

Housing associations are not usually able to help at short notice or in emergencies but may be prepared to put your name on a waiting list. If their lists are closed, you will probably only be considered if you are put forward (nominated) by your local authority or another referral agency. In some circumstances, housing associations may consider buying your home and either leave you in it or rehouse you elsewhere. You will get less for your home than if you sell it on the open market, because an occupied house is worth less than an empty one. However, you will be getting somewhere to live out of the arrangement. If you do this, you must make sure that you will get enough money to clear all your debts.

You may be able to persuade a housing association to buy your home from you and to resell part of it back to you under a shared ownership scheme (see page 7). Your local authority or Citizens' Advice Bureau will be able to give you the names of housing associations in your area.

If you rent accommodation privately or from a housing association or the local authority, you will be able to claim housing benefit provided your income and capital are not too high. See page 24 for more about the housing benefit system.

Approach your local housing authority

Your local authority may be able to help you in a number of ways, so go to them as soon as possible and explain your situation. **A local authority may:**

- □ **give you advice.** Many local authorities have housing advice centres where people can be helped to sort out their difficulties;

- □ **rehouse you.** They may only be able to put your name on a waiting list, and you should do this even if there seems no immediate need. Different local authorities have different policies for helping people in mortgage difficulties, so ask what they might do for you;

- □ **accept you as homeless and rehouse you.**

HOMELESSNESS AND LOCAL AUTHORITIES

If you are already homeless or are likely to become homeless within 28 days after you report your situation to your local authority, then you have certain legal rights under the Housing Act 1985, Part III (in Scotland, the Housing (Scotland) Act 1987). This puts a legal obligation on local authorities to provide accommodation for people who fulfil certain conditions. These conditions are detailed below with suggestions for what action you should take.

- ☐ **You must be homeless.** You do not have to have no roof over your head to be homeless. People who have accommodation but no legal right to occupy it are also homeless, including those whose homes have been repossessed. Others who are homeless include people who are living in accommodation which it is unreasonable for them to continue to occupy (for instance, because it is overcrowded or in a state of disrepair); people who have accommodation but are unable to secure entry to it; and people who have had to leave their accommodation because of the threat of violence. Go to your local authority as soon as you know that you will be homeless. They have a duty to begin investigations if you will be homeless within 28 days and must provide accommodation if you are actually homeless and are in priority need.

- ☐ **You must be in priority need.** This means you have dependent children; or any member of your household is pregnant; or any member of your household is vulnerable because of old age, illness or disability or for some other special reason; or you are homeless because of fire or flood or some other disaster.

- ☐ **You must not have made yourself homeless intentionally.** You are intentionally homeless if you deliberately do, or fail to do, something which results in your homelessness if it would have been reasonable for you to have continued to occupy the property. However, if your homelessness results from something done in good faith or because you were unaware that there were any alternatives, you should not be judged intentionally homeless. The Code of Guidance (paragraph 7.4) on homelessness says:

    Generally, it should not be considered deliberate where an applicant has lost her/his home or was obliged to sell it because s/he got into mortgage arrears because of real financial difficulties – for example because s/he became unemployed or ill or suffered greatly reduced earnings or family breakdown – and could genuinely not keep up the rent payments or loan payments even after claiming benefits and for whom no further financial help is available. In the case of mortgagors, authorities should look at the applicant's ability to pay the mortgage commitment, when it was taken on, given her/his financial circumstances at the time (7.4(b)).

It should also generally not be considered deliberate where an owner occupier, who is faced with foreclosure or possession proceedings to which there is no defence, sells before the mortgagee recovers possession through the courts or surrenders the property to the lender (7.5(c)).

- **Even if you are intentionally homeless, you are entitled to accommodation for a reasonable period if you are in priority need.** The Code of Guidance on homelessness does not have the same force as the Act, but it might be helpful to your case. A similar Code of Guidance has been issued by the Secretary of State for Scotland. The latest version was issued in 1991. If you are applying as a homeless person to the local authority it is important to give the local authority as much financial information as possible detailing your circumstances to show that you could genuinely not afford to make payments. You could draw up your own financial statement (see page 75 and Appendix 8) to make it clear what your income and expenditure was during the time you were in difficulties.

If you are homeless or about to become homeless, contact one of the organisations listed in Appendix 7 for advice.

There are a number of additional points to remember:

- Your local authority is responsible for your belongings as well as for you, even if it has put you in temporary accommodation.

- Your local authority must provide accommodation if you need it until it has completed any necessary investigation.

- You are entitled to written notification of any decision it takes about you under this Act. If the decision is unfavourable, the local authority must state its reasons. If this happens to you, it may be possible to challenge the decision, so get advice – see Appendix 7.

- If your local authority decides that it has a duty to rehouse you, it does not have to discharge this duty by providing you with a council tenancy. It can provide you with a tenancy with a housing association or with a private landlord. It can even take steps (such as guaranteeing a mortgage or nominating you to shared ownership scheme) to rehouse you in owner-occupied accommodation if this is appropriate.

Changes to the legislation

This describes the law affecting homeless people at present. But on 18 July

1994 *the government announced its intention to fundamentally change this law*. In England and Wales, if the government succeeds in its intention to pass this legislation in the 1994/95 session of parliament, it will become law while this book is still current. The most important proposed changes are as follows:

- ☐ You will not have a right to assistance unless you have no accommodation available, however temporary or insecure. This will not, however, apply if you are applying as homeless from a short-stay hostel or a women's refuge.

- ☐ The local authority will have no duty to provide you with permanent rehousing. You will receive temporary accommodation for a minimum of one, and a maximum of two, years. Much of this accommodation is likely to be in expensive privately rented properties where you will have few rights to tackle problems such as disrepair, although you will be entitled to claim housing benefit. Instead of permanently rehousing you as a homeless person, the local authority will place you on the general housing waiting list.

- ☐ After two years you will only be entitled to further temporary accommodation if you are still in priority need and unintentionally homeless and there is still no other accommodation available to you, however temporary or insecure.

- ☐ People applying as homeless who have been asked to leave their accommodation by friends or relatives may find it more difficult to be accepted as homeless.

In Scotland, a Consultation Paper – 'Tackling Homelessness' – has been produced by the Scottish Office, canvassing opinion on several of the above options. To date, the Scottish Office has not yet indicated the outcome of the consultation.

We hope that, using this guide, many people will keep their existing flats and houses and not have to rely on homelessness legislation to find somewhere that they can call home. But this legislation remains an important safety net and these proposals would considerably weaken the rights of homeless people. The government received nearly 10,000 submissions from local authorities, other organisations and individuals opposing these changes. Hopefully, a way into decent permanent rehousing for homeless people will be preserved as a result of this opposition.

APPENDIX ONE

How to work out your mortgage repayments

HOW TO WORK OUT YOUR MONTHLY PAYMENTS ON A REPAYMENT MORTGAGE

The tables printed below will enable you to work out the total monthly costs of mortgages of different amounts over different terms. The monthly payments include interest and capital.

Note that the longer the term, the lower the repayment. This is because repayment of capital is spread over more years. The change from 15 to 20 years makes more difference than the change from 25 to 30 years.

Because most mortgages receive government subsidy through tax relief at source (MIRAS), payments on the first £30,000 will be lower. MIRAS is received at 20 per cent from April 1994 and at 15 per cent from April 1995. This means that your mortgage payments will increase in April 1995.

Example:

If your mortgage interest rate is 8%, the net rate of interest that you actually pay after receiving MIRAS will be:

| From April 1994 | 6.4% (8% – 20% of 8%) |
| From April 1995 | 6.8% (8% – 15% of 8%) |

Your payments consist of both interest payments and repayment of capital. Rates vary from time to time and the tables below give the cost for different rates of interest and different repayment periods. The figure given is the monthly repayment in pounds you make on each £1,000 you have borrowed.

Table 1
Net repayments on the first £30,000 until April 1995

Actual rate	Interest rate you pay after MIRAS at 20%	Monthly repayment per £1,000 borrowed			
		Repayment period			
		15 yrs	20 yrs	25 yrs	30 yrs
%	%	£ p	£ p	£ p	£ p
10.0	8.0	9.74	8.49	7.81	7.41
9.5	7.6	9.50	8.24	7.55	7.13
9.0	7.2	9.27	7.99	7.29	6.86
8.5	6.8	9.04	7.75	7.03	6.59
8.0	6.4	8.81	7.51	6.77	6.32
7.5	6.0	8.59	7.27	6.52	6.06
7.0	5.6	8.36	7.04	6.28	5.80
6.5	5.2	8.14	6.81	6.04	5.55
6.0	4.8	7.93	6.58	5.80	5.30
5.5	4.4	7.71	6.36	5.57	5.06
5.0	4.0	7.50	6.14	5.34	4.82

Table 2
Net repayments on the first £30,000 after April 1995

Actual rate	Interest rate you pay after MIRAS at 15%	Monthly repayment per £1,000 borrowed			
		Repayment period			
		15 yrs	20 yrs	25 yrs	30 yrs
%	%	£ p	£ p	£ p	£ p
10.0	8.5	10.04	8.81	8.15	7.76
9.5	8.1	9.80	8.56	7.88	7.48
9.0	7.65	9.53	8.27	7.58	7.16
8.5	7.25	9.30	7.75	7.03	6.59
8.0	6.8	9.04	7.75	7.03	6.59
7.5	6.4	8.81	7.51	6.77	6.32
7.0	5.95	8.56	7.24	6.49	6.03
6.5	5.55	8.33	7.01	6.25	5.77
6.0	5.1	8.09	6.75	5.98	5.49
5.5	4.7	7.87	6.52	5.74	5.24
5.0	4.25	7.63	6.27	5.48	4.97

APPENDIX ONE 143

Table 3
Repayments on mortgages outside MIRAS

Interest rate	Monthly repayment per £1,000 borrowed			
	Repayment period			
%	15 yrs £ p	20 yrs £ p	25 yrs £ p	30 yrs £ p
10.0	10.96	9.79	9.19	8.84
9.5	10.65	9.46	8.83	8.48
9.0	10.34	9.13	8.49	8.12
8.5	10.04	8.81	8.15	7.76
8.0	9.74	8.49	7.81	7.41
7.5	9.45	8.18	7.48	7.03
7.0	9.15	7.87	7.16	6.72
6.5	8.87	7.57	6.84	6.39
6.0	8.59	7.27	6.52	6.06
5.5	8.31	6.98	6.22	5.74
5.0	8.03	6.69	5.92	5.43

How to use the tables

A: To calculate payments on a repayment mortgage

Example 1:
If you have a £50,000 mortgage in MIRAS over 25 years at 7.5%, use Table 1 to find out how much you will pay per £1,000 borrowed on the first £30,000 (for which you receive MIRAS):

£6.52 x 30 = £195.60 per month, which are your repayments on the first £30,000.

Table 2 shows that from April 1995 (assuming that interest rates remain unchanged) you will pay:

£6.77 x 30 = £203.10 per month.

To this you must add the amount you will pay on the remaining £20,000 outside MIRAS. Using Table 3 you find that this is:

£7.48 x 20 = £149.60 per month.

So your total monthly payments will be:

Until April 1995:	£195.60 – inside MIRAS
	+ £149.60 – outside MIRAS
	£345.20
After April 1995:	£203.10 – inside MIRAS
	+ £149.60 – outside MIRAS
	£352.70

B: To work out your interest payments

You will need to do this if you have an endowment, pension or repayment mortgage. In the case of a repayment mortgage, working out your interest payments will enable you to calculate your capital repayments.

You will need to know how much you owe your lender.

- ☐ If you have an endowment or pension mortgage, this will be the amount you borrowed initially (plus any arrears which have been capitalised).

- ☐ If you have a repayment mortgage this will fall as you make repayments. Ask your lender how much is still owed or check your most recent statement.

Example 2:

You have a £30,000 endowment mortgage in MIRAS at 7.5% interest. Before April 1995 the net interest rate will be 6% (Table 1 columns 1 and 2). So the annual interest payable will be:

£30,000 x 6% = £1,800

Your monthly interest payments will be:

£1,800 ÷ 12 = £150

After April 1995 the net interest rate will be 6.4% (Table 2 columns 1 and 2). So your annual interest will be:

£30,000 x 6.4% = £1,920

Your monthly interest payments will be:

£1,920 ÷ 12 = £160

(You will need to add your endowment premiums to the interest to give your total monthly payments.)

APPENDIX ONE   145

Example 3:
If you have an endowment mortgage for £50,000 at 7.5% the payments on the first £30,000 will be exactly the same as in example 2.

You will need to add to this the payments on the remaining £20,000 at the full 7.5%, your annual payments will be:
  £20,000 x 7.5% = £1,500

Your monthly payments on £20,000 outside MIRAS will be:
  £1,500 12 = £125
So your total monthly interest payments will be:
  Before April 1995:   £150 – inside MIRAS
              +£125 – outside MIRAS
              £275
  After April 1995:   £160 – inside MIRAS
              +£125 – outside MIRAS
              £285

C: To work out your capital repayments on a repayment mortgage

You will need to work these out, for instance, if you are on income support to establish which proportion of your mortgage the Benefits Agency will not cover.

Example 4:
If your mortgage was a repayment mortgage for £50,000 over 25 years at an interest rate of 7.5% – the same as in example 1 – and you had repaid £20,000, you would still have to pay interest on the remaining £30,000. (This would be the same as in example 2.)

So, until April 1995, your capital repayments will be your total repayments (£345.20) minus the interest on £30,000 outstanding at 6% net interest after MIRAS – ie:

  £345.20 total repayment
  £150.00 interest payment
  £192.00 capital repayment

APPENDIX TWO

How to calculate family credit

You will get the same amount of family credit throughout the six months of the award (see page 15). The figures given below are for the year April 1994 to April 1995.

THE CALCULATION

To work out how much family credit you qualify for, follow these steps:

(i) Work out your maximum family credit

Add together the child credits for each of your children, according to their age, and one adult credit. (You only include one adult credit, whether you have a partner, or are a lone parent.)

Adult credit	£44.30
Child credits (one for each child)	
Under 11	£11.20
11-15	£18.55
16-17	£23.05
18	£32.20

No allowance is given for a child who has:

- ☐ capital of over £3,000;
- ☐ a weekly income (excluding maintenance) which is greater than her/his allowance;
- ☐ been in hospital or local authority residential accommodation for the 52 weeks prior to your claim because of physical or mental illness or handicap.

(ii) Work out your income

See page 18 for how to do this and for what to include in your calculation.

Remember, from October 1994 you can deduct up to £40 childcare costs from your earnings (see page 19).

(iii) Compare your income with the threshold level

Until April 1995 this will be £71.70.

☐ If your net income is below the threshold, then you will be entitled to maximum family credit (see (i) above).

☐ If your income is above the threshold:
 – work out the excess over the threshold;
 – calculate 70% of the excess;
 – deduct this from the maximum family credit to find the amount of family credit that will be paid.

Example

Ms Jones is a lone parent with two children of 12 and 10. Her net earnings are £110 per week (after taking into account, among other things, childcare costs of £40), and she receives child benefit and one parent benefit.

Maximum family credit

Adult credit	£44.30
Child credits	
12-year-old	£18.55
10-year-old	£11.20
	£74.05

Income

Ms Jones' income = £110 per week.
(Child benefit and one parent benefit are ignored for the purpose of calculating her income.)

Final calculation

☐ Ms Jones' income is £38.30 over the threshold (£110 - £71.70).
☐ 70% of this excess is £26.81;
☐ the family credit payable is:

 £74.05 (maximum family credit)
 minus £26.81 (70% of excess income)
 £47.24 total family credit payable weekly

APPENDIX THREE

Income support rates until April 1995

PERSONAL ALLOWANCES

Different rates are paid for single people, couples and lone parents, with additions for children according to age.

Single people
Under 18	£27.50
Under 18 (in certain circumstances)	£36.15
18-24	£36.15
25 or over	£45.70

Single parents
Under 18	£27.50
Under 18 (in certain circumstances)	£36.15
18 or over	£45.70

Couples
If one or both of the couple are under 18, the personal allowance may be lower – see CPAG's *National Welfare Benefits Handbook*.	£71.70

Dependent children
Under 11	£15.65
11-15	£23.00
16-17	£27.50
18	£36.15

PREMIUMS

These are fixed additional amounts paid to specific groups of people. For detailed advice about whether you might qualify for one or more premiums, see Appendix 7. The rules are quite complicated. There are similar rules for premiums for housing benefit and council tax benefit.

Family premium £10.05

You will be entitled to this premium if you have at least one child or young person (certain 16-18-year-olds) living with you. Only one premium is paid per family.

Disabled child premium £19.45

If you have a disabled child who is receiving disability living allowance, or is registered blind, you will be able to get the disabled child premium. You won't get this premium if the child has more than £3,000 in savings of her/his own. One premium is paid for each disabled child.

Lone parent premium £5.10

You will be entitled to this premium if you are a lone parent, and claim benefit for at least one child.

Pensioner premium

	lower rate	enhanced rate
single	£18.25	£20.35
couple	£27.55	£30.40

If you or your partner (if you have one) are aged between 60 and 74, you will be entitled to a premium at the lower rate. The enhanced rate is payable if you or your partner are aged 75-79 inclusive.

Higher pensioner premium

single	£24.70
couple	£35.30

You will be entitled to this premium if either you or your partner (if you have one) are aged 80 or over, *or* if one of you is aged 60-79 and either of you is getting a qualifying benefit (such as attendance allowance), has an invalid car or is registered blind, *or* if you or your partner were getting a disability premium within eight weeks of your 60th birthday and have been entitled to income support ever since (you are allowed breaks of up to eight weeks).

Disability premium

single	£19.45
couple	£27.80

If you or your partner (if you have one) are getting attendance allowance, disability living allowance, disability working allowance, have an invalid car, or are registered blind or are receiving invalidity benefit or severe disablement allowance, you will be entitled to this premium. You will also be entitled if you (or your partner – if s/he is the claimant) have been incapable of work for

28 weeks. It may be worth changing which of you is the claimant if one of you is too ill or disabled to work (see page 28). In all cases, you or your partner must be under 60. You get the couple rate if either of you qualifies.

Severe disability premium   single £34.30
                                couple £34.30 (one qualifies)
                                couple £68.60 (both qualify)

If you are a **single claimant,** you will be entitled to this if you are receiving attendance allowance, or the higher or middle rate care component of disability living allowance, and you have no non-dependants over 18 living with you and there is no one receiving invalid care allowance for looking after you (see page 40 for the meaning of 'non-dependant').

For **couples**, both of you must be receiving attendance allowance, or the middle or higher rate care component of disability living allowance, have no non-dependants over 18 living with you, and there must be no one getting invalid care allowance for looking after both of you. If your partner is registered blind, s/he need not be getting attendance allowance, etc, but you will then be treated as a single claimant. If you both meet these conditions, but someone receives invalid care allowance for caring for one of you, then you will still receive the single rate of premium. Otherwise you will get the couple rate.

Note that if the non-dependant is her/himself getting attendance allowance, etc, is registered blind or has just moved in as a carer, s/he does not disqualify you. Paid carers engaged by a charity or voluntary organisation who charge you are not 'non-dependants'.

Carer's premium   £12.40

You will be entitled to this premium if you receive invalid care allowance, or would receive it if it did not overlap with some other benefit you are receiving. The premium is paid for each person who is entitled to invalid care allowance, so you may get it for your partner.

Which premium?

You can receive the following premiums on top of any others you receive:
- disabled child premium
- carer's premium
- family premium
- severe disability premium

If you qualify for more than one of the other premiums you will receive whichever is the highest.

APPENDIX FOUR

Rules about savings and capital for income support, family credit, council tax benefit, housing benefit and disability working allowance

The rules used by the Benefits Agency and local authorities to assess your savings or capital are almost the same for the five 'income-related' benefits – income support (IS), family credit (FC), council tax benefit (CTB), housing benefit (HB), and disability working allowance (DWA). There are, however, some differences. It is best to get advice from one of the agencies listed in Appendix 7.

GENERAL RULES

If you and your partner have more than £8,000 in savings or other capital (£16,000 for CTB, HB and DWA) you won't then qualify for these benefits at all. If you have less than £3,000, they are ignored completely. Any savings between £3,000 and £8,000 (£16,000 for CTB, HB and DWA) are assumed to give you an income of £1 per week for each £250 (or part of £250) over £3,000 that you have. This is called 'tariff income'.

If any of your children have savings of their own, these will not be counted as yours. However, if a child has savings of more than £3,000, you will receive no benefit for her/him (but you will still get the family premium and lone parent premium, if you qualify – see Chapter three).

WHAT IS INCLUDED IN CAPITAL?

Capital includes, among other things:

☐ money in bank or building society accounts;

☐ premium bonds;

- ☐ unit trusts;
- ☐ stocks and shares;
- ☐ lump-sum redundancy payments;
- ☐ savings in cash;
- ☐ property which you don't normally live in.

WHAT CAPITAL IS IGNORED?

Some capital is ignored, including:

- ☐ the value of the home you normally live in;
- ☐ the value of your former home for 26 weeks after you leave due to divorce or separation;
- ☐ a property you have bought and intend to occupy within 26 weeks;*
- ☐ money from the sale of a house which is to be used to buy another home within 26 weeks* (this includes where you surrender a leasehold interest before it comes to an end – ie, you give it back to the freeholder);
- ☐ the value of premises occupied wholly or partly by:
  - your partner (if the law still regards you as living together) or a relative, who in either case is 60 or over, or unable to work, or disabled;
  - someone the law regarded as your partner when you were living together (but not if you are now divorced or estranged). An example of this situation might be if you had to move into a residential care home leaving your partner at home;
- ☐ the value of a house neither you nor your partner live in. This will be ignored for 26 weeks* after you start:
  - to take reasonable steps to sell the property; *or*
  - to take legal action to occupy the property; *or*
  - to carry out essential repairs or alterations to enable you to occupy the house;
- ☐ business assets of a self-employed person. If the business has ceased, they are ignored for a reasonable time to enable you to dispose of them;

---

* These time limits may be extended if it is reasonable to do so.

- compensation for loss or damage to the home or possessions – for example, insurance payments – will be ignored for 26 weeks* provided you use the money for repair or replacement;

- loans or gifts of money for essential repairs or improvements are ignored for 26 weeks;*

- arrears of attendance allowance, mobility allowance, disability living allowance or a means-tested benefit (for 52 weeks);

- the value of property subject to a tenancy. However, the Court of Appeal will rule in December 1994 whether this should indeed be ignored. Rent which you receive from tenanted property is counted as capital, not income;

- personal possessions, unless they were bought in order to claim more benefit;

- surrender value of an annuity or life insurance policy (including an endowment policy);

- capital in a trust fund which comes from a payment for personal injuries;

- social fund payments (see page 49);

- tax refund of mortgage interest relief.

This is only a brief breakdown of what the rules say. If you are in any doubt about these rules get advice from one of the organisations in Appendix 7.

---

* These time limits may be extended if it is reasonable to do so.

Specimen letters requesting a loan for repairs

IF YOU ARE WORKING

The Manager
Westgate Building Society
High Street
Westgate

12 Park Road
Westgate

Account No: 246853

Dear Mr Brown   Date:

I need to raise some money to do major repairs to my house. I will not be able to get a grant from the local authority so I will have to raise the money myself. A surveyor has told me which repairs are needed and I enclose a copy of his report. I have been able to get estimates of the cost of putting in the damp-proof course and the rewiring. These two items will come to about £2,000, and the builder who came to see it thought that other work, costing a further £800, needed to be done. I will send you copies of the estimates as soon as I have them.

    I would like an additional loan of £3,000 because that would then give me some extra in case any problems were discovered. It would also help me to buy the materials to redecorate (I would do that work myself). My mortgage payments are £350 a month plus £7.50 for my mortgage protection policy. My council tax is equivalent to £50 a month and we spend about £40 a month on gas/electricity. That adds up to about £447.50.

    I calculated that borrowing another £3,000 over the 20 years that my mortgage still has to run would cost another £32.43 a month which would take my costs up to £479.93 a month.

    At the moment, I take home £800 a month, but we have just agreed our annual pay rise and I will be getting nearly £830 next month. My wife also gets £17.45 child benefit a week (£75.61 a month). I have about £500 in the bank which I could use for the repairs, but I know there will be legal fees, etc, and will need my savings for those.

Yours sincerely

James Green

(You could alternatively enclose a financial statement showing how you can manage payments – see Appendix 8).

IF YOU RECEIVE INCOME SUPPORT

The Manager　　　　　　　　　　　　　　　　　　　　　23 Bank St
Westgate Building Society　　　　　　　　　　　　　　　　Westgate
High Street
Westgate　　　　　　　　　　　　　　　　　　Account No: 7532345

Dear Mr Brown　　　　　　　　　　　　　　　Date:

I need to raise some money to do urgent repairs to my house. The roof is leaking and several of the window frames are badly rotted. I am enclosing copies of two estimates which you can see put the cost at about £3,000. I have applied to my local authority for a repairs grant. They have said I am probably eligible but they cannot let me know for a few weeks. If I receive a grant from them, I would only need to borrow £1,500.

I have spoken to my Benefits Agency office, which is willing to meet payments on an additional loan of either amount and I enclose a letter from the manager confirming that. My Benefits Agency office will also pay the interest directly to you.

As you know, I work part-time and am meeting the capital payments out of the part of my income that the Benefits Agency ignores. I have worked out that I would still be able to afford to do that if I borrowed more.

I am concerned about any fees that will be charged and would be grateful if you could give me an estimate of the costs involved in an additional mortgage.

Yours sincerely

Mary Jones

Legal aid

If you have severe financial problems you may need a solicitor to advise you and, if necessary, to represent you in court, or arrange for a barrister to represent you. You will almost certainly need professional legal advice if you and your partner are separating.

HOW TO FIND A SOLICITOR

Your local citizens advice bureau or advice centre will be able to give you the names of solicitors who specialise in the areas of law on which you need advice, and who operate the legal aid scheme.

HOW MUCH WILL IT COST?

There are two main kinds of non-criminal legal aid, the 'green form scheme' (in Scotland, 'pink form') and help under a 'legal aid certificate'. The rules for working out whether you qualify for help are different for the two schemes. Another difference is that, with the green form scheme, your solicitor works out immediately whether you are eligible. With help under a legal aid certificate, the financial calculations are made by the Benefits Agency.

The green form scheme is now non-contributory – in other words, either you qualify for free help or you do not qualify at all. In Scotland, the pink form scheme is still means-tested and you may have a contribution to pay. With legal aid itself, however, you may have to pay a contribution if you have a certain amount of income or capital. It is an annual contribution – the longer the case takes, the more you pay.

Although fewer people qualify for legal aid these days, it is still worth enquiring. What counts is how much *disposable* income and capital you have. You are allowed to make various deductions from your income and capital – for example, deductions for dependants and work expenses from your income. Your home does *not* count as part of your disposable capital.

THE GREEN FORM SCHEME

The official name for this is the 'legal advice and assistance scheme'. Under the scheme, those who come within the financial limits can obtain at least two hours of advice and assistance on practically any area of the law free of charge. This is increased to at least three hours in cases of undefended divorce or judicial separation. If you are getting income support (see page 28), family credit (see page 14) or disability working allowance (see page 19), you will qualify automatically, unless you have too much capital.

The scheme allows your solicitor to write letters, negotiate on your behalf and obtain advice from a barrister about your case. However, you cannot, apart from one or two exceptions, get help with the cost of representation at a court or tribunal – although under the scheme, your solicitor can give you advice on how to conduct your case in person.

Under the scheme, solicitors *can* do more than two (or three) hours of work if they obtain prior authority from the legal aid board.

Note that some solicitors offer a free first interview in accident cases.

The legal aid board is currently examining other methods of providing legal advice and assistance, including whether advice agencies could provide help of the kind which is currently provided by solicitors under the green form scheme.

In Scotland, the equivalent scheme is the 'advice and assistance scheme' (pink form). As indicated above, it is means-tested. If you are on income support or family credit, you can get free advice. In other cases, you will need to make a contribution.

LEGAL AID UNDER A LEGAL AID CERTIFICATE

This is available for costs that will be incurred in connection with proceedings in a civil court. Your solicitor will help you to fill in the application form. It will normally take a few weeks for the application to be processed, and it will not be possible to start court proceedings until the certificate is granted. However, in urgent cases – for example, to obtain an injunction to exclude a violent spouse from the matrimonial home – an application for emergency legal aid can be made. In cases of extreme urgency, a solicitor can request an emergency certificate over the telephone.

To qualify for help, you have to pass two tests:

- ☐ You must come within the financial limits, as assessed by the Benefits Agency. These change fairly frequently. You can check the current levels at your local citizens advice bureau, who will probably be able to give you a good idea as to whether you qualify and, roughly, what your contribution, if any, would be. If you are getting income support, you qualify automatically (with no contribution to pay). You should note that, if you are living with your partner in a heterosexual relationship, and your dispute is not with her/him, your income and capital will be added together in working out whether you qualify for help. If your child needs to bring a case, her/his means are looked at separately.

☐ You have to have reasonable grounds for taking or defending the action. This will be decided by the legal aid board on the basis of the case put to them in the application form, and the supporting papers enclosed. They will not be pre-judging the matter – that is not their job – but rather coming to a decision as to whether it is reasonable for public funds to be spent in giving you financial assistance.

In Scotland, the Scottish Legal Aid Board performs a similar function.

THE STATUTORY CHARGE

There is one particular feature of legal aid which it is vital for anyone who seeks legal aid to understand. If you recover or are allowed to keep money or property in dispute (including, for example, a house), then you may have to pay legal costs incurred on your behalf which are more than any contribution you have had to pay (see page 156). You would have to pay the costs out of that money or property. Normally, the costs of the winning party, or at any rate the bulk of the costs, are paid by the losing party. If the losing party does pay all your costs, there is no problem. However, if the losing party is also on legal aid, s/he will usually not be ordered to pay your costs. This means that, in effect, you may well end up paying all your legal costs, even though you may have been assessed as having to make a nil contribution. Anyone on legal aid should therefore be aware of the 'statutory charge', as this feature of the scheme is called. Solicitors have a duty to explain how the charge operates to their legally-aided clients, and you should make sure that a full explanation is given to you.

Special rules apply where there have been matrimonial or similar proceedings: here the first £2,500 of a lump sum or property adjustment order is exempt from the charge.

Where it is a house, which is to be used as a home for you or your dependants, that has been recovered or retained, the legal aid board has discretion in these sorts of proceedings not to insist on immediate payment of the sum due to them, and also discretion to transfer the charge to different property. Similarly, if you win a sum of money which is to be used to buy a home for you or your dependants, the charge can again be postponed. In these cases, it is the practice to wait until the house is sold before recovering the money. Again, the legal aid board may agree to transfer the charge to a different house. Obviously, the equity in the second house (in other words, how much the house is worth after deducting the statutory charge and any mortgage) must be sufficient to cover the amount owed to the legal aid board. Simple interest is added to the amount outstanding until payment.

There have been a number of very grim cases in recent years where an ex-spouse on legal aid who has been involved in a prolonged and expensive dispute over property with the former spouse, has been left with very little of the sum awarded to her/him because of the way in which the statutory charge operates. It is always worth making every effort to negotiate a settlement prior to a court hearing rather than fighting the matter out in court. Though the court might award you a somewhat greater sum than has been offered to you to settle, you could still end up getting much less, because of the extra costs you incurred in taking the matter to court - costs that may have to be paid out of the sum awarded to you.

The statutory charge does not apply in cases about your entitlement to social security benefits.

APPENDIX SEVEN

Useful addresses

Advice agencies

If you would like further advice on any of the subjects covered in this guide, the following local organisations may be able to help:

- a law centre;
- a citizens advice bureau;
- an advice centre;
- a money or consumer advice centre;
- a housing aid centre;
- a local authority welfare rights department.

You can find out the details of these agencies from the telephone directory, local authority offices or libraries.

If you are unable to find help in your area, one of the following groups may be able to advise you, or refer you to someone who can.

SHAC (The London Housing Aid Centre)
Kingsbourne House
229-231 High Holborn
London WC1V 7DA
Tel: 071-404 6929

(Gives advice on all problems to do with housing to people in London.)

Shelter Housing Aid
88 Old Street
London EC1V 9AX
Tel: 071-253 0202

(Shelter runs a network of Housing Aid Centres outside London; contact its head office for details of the nearest HAC.)

National Debtline
318 Summer Lane
Birmingham B19 3RL
Tel: 021-359 8501

(Specialises in advice and information on all forms of debts, especially arrears of housing costs and business debts.)

APPENDIX SEVEN

Law Centres Federation
Duchess House
18-19 Warren Street
London W1P 5DB
Tel: 071-387 8570

Federation of Independent Advice Centres
13 Stockwell Road
London SW9 9AU
Tel: 071-274 1893

National Association of Citizens Advice Bureaux
115/123 Pentonville Road
London N1 9LZ
Tel: 071-833 2181

Gingerbread
49 Wellington Street
London WC2E 7BN
Tel: 071-240 0953

(A national organisation for lone parents, with local branches. Offers general advice and can refer on to specialist agencies.)

Women's Aid Federation (England)
PO Box 391
Bristol BS99 7WS
Tel: 0272-633542

Welsh Women's Aid
38-48 Crwys Road
Cardiff CF2 4NN
Tel: 0222 390 874

(Refers women, with or without children, who need to leave home due to physical, emotional or sexual abuse, to refuges. Gives advice on injunctions, divorce, housing, social security. Referrals made to sympathetic solicitors or local women's aid groups.)

Other organisations mentioned in this guide:

Building Societies' Association
3 Savile Row
London W1X 1AF
Tel: 071-437 0655

Child Support Agency (CSA)

There are five CSA centres in England, Wales and Scotland; they can be contacted through the CSA's advice line: 0345-133133

Council of Mortgage Lenders
3 Savile Row
London W1X 1AF
Tel: 071-437 0655

DSS/Benefits Agency
Family Credit Unit
Government Buildings
Warbreck Hill
Blackpool FY2 0YF
Tel: 0253-500050

DSS/Benefits Agency
Disability Working Allowance Unit
2 The Pavilion
Preston PR2 2GN
Tel: 0772-883300

Benefits Agency Advice Lines:
- benefit enquiry line: 0800 555 666
  (Minicom: 0800 243 355)
- disability benefits: 0800 882 200
- family credit: 0800 500 222

District Land Registry Office
HM Land Registry
32 Lincoln's Inn Fields
London WC2A 3PH
Tel: 071-917 8888

Energy Action Grants Agency
Freepost
PO Box 1NG
Newcastle Upon Tyne NE99 2BP
Freephone 0800-181667

Land Charges Registry
Burrington Way
Plymouth PL5 3LP
Tel: 0752-779831

Law Society
113 Chancery Lane
London WC2A 1PL
Tel: 071-242 1222

Leaseholder Enfranchisement
Advisory Service
616 Maddox St
London W1R 9PN
Tel: 071-493 3116

Local Government Ombudsman
21 Queen Anne's Gate
London SW1H 9BU
Tel: 071-222 5622

Scotland
Princes House
5 Shandwick Place
Edinburgh EH2 4RE
Tel: 031-229 4472

Wales
Derwen House
Court Road
Bridgend CF31 1BN
Tel: 0656-661325

Office of the Building Societies
Ombudsman
35-37 Grosvenor Gardens
London SW1X 7AW
Tel: 071-931 0044

Housing Corporation
149 Tottenham Court Road
London W1P 0BN
Tel: 071-387 9466

Scottish organisations

SHELTER (Scotland)
8 Hampton Terrace
Edinburgh EH12 5JD
Tel: 031-313 1550

Money Advice Scotland
43 Broughton Street
Edinburgh EH1 3JU

Citizens Advice Scotland
26 George Square
Edinburgh EH8 9LD
Tel: 031-667 0156

Scottish Association of Law Centres
c/o Legal Services Agency
11th Floor
Fleming House
134 Renfrew Street
Glasgow G3 6ST

Law Society of Scotland
26 Drumsheugh Gardens
Edinburgh EH3 7YR
Tel: 031-226 7411

APPENDIX EIGHT

Financial statements – example

INCOME SHEET

WAGES	AMOUNT	
	NET	GROSS
1.		
2.		
3.		
4.		
TOTAL		

BENEFITS	AMOUNT
1.	
2.	
3.	
4.	
TOTAL	

OTHER INCOME	AMOUNT
OCCUPATIONAL PENSIONS 1. 2.	
MAINTENANCE	
INCOME FROM LODGERS/SUB-TENANTS	
OTHER WEEKLY INCOME – GIVE SOURCE 1. 2.	
IRREGULAR INCOME – GIVE SOURCE 1. 2.	
INCOME ON SAVINGS (IF TREATED AS WEEKLY INCOME) 1. 2.	
OTHER INCOME – GIVE SOURCE 1. 2.	
TOTAL	

	AMOUNT
TOTAL WEEKLY INCOME	

EXPENDITURE SHEET

HOUSING COSTS	AMOUNT
MORTGAGE PAYMENTS	
MORTGAGE PROT. INS.	
ENDOWMENT PREM	
2ND MORTGAGE	
3RD MORTGAGE	
SERVICE CHARGE	
GROUND RENT	
OTHER INSURANCES	
REPAIRS	
COUNCIL TAX	
TOTAL	

OTHER PAYMENTS	AMOUNT
OTHER LOAN PAYMENTS	
HIRE PURCHASE	
CREDIT CARDS	
STORE CARDS	
TOTAL	

HOUSEKEEPING	AMOUNT
FOOD	
MILK	
CLEANING MATERIALS	
TELEPHONE	
TV RENTAL	
TV LICENCE	
PET FOOD	
NEWSPAPERS	
KIDS' POCKET MONEY	
OTHER ITEMS	
TOTAL	

FUEL COSTS	AMOUNT
GAS	
ELECTRICITY	
COAL	
CALOR GAS	
PARAFFIN/FUEL OIL	
CENTRAL HEATING	
SERVICE	
INSURANCE	
TOTAL	

TRAVEL	AMOUNT
TO WORK	
TO SCHOOL	
SHOPPING	
VISITS	
TOTAL	

CAR	AMOUNT
ROAD TAX	
INSURANCE	
M.O.T.	
REPAIRS	
PETROL & OIL	
TOTAL	

OTHER ITEMS	AMOUNT
CLOTHING	
SCHOOL MEALS	
FURNITURE	
OTHER HOUSEHOLD GOODS	
CHILDCARE	
TOOLS FOR WORK	
ENTERTAINMENTS	
MAINTENANCE PAYMENTS	
FINES	
OTHER	
TOTAL	

	AMOUNT
TOTAL WEEKLY EXPENDITURE	

APPENDIX NINE

Useful publications

WELFARE BENEFITS AND CHILD SUPPORT

National Welfare Benefits Handbook (1994/95 edition), price £7.95 (£2.65 for claimants) p&p incl, and *Rights Guide to Non-Means-Tested Social Security Benefits* (1994/95 edition), price £6.95 (£2.65 for claimants) p&p incl. Both books are available from CPAG Ltd, 1-5 Bath Street, London EC1V 9PY. So is CPAG's *Child Support Handbook* (1994/95 edition), price £6.95 (£2.45 for claimants), p&p incl. All three books are updated annually. CPAG also publishes *Council Tax Handbook*, by Martin Ward, price £7.95 p&p incl.

HOUSING

SHAC publishes a wide range of detailed housing rights guides. These include: *Housing Benefit/Council Tax Benefit Guide* (published jointly with Institute of Housing, price £10.95); *Housing Rights Guide* (price £10.95); and two guides on the housing rights of married and unmarried women (price £7.95 each). Contact SHAC's publications department on 071-404 7447 for more information.

PUBLICATIONS FROM OTHER ORGANISATIONS

Department of Environment Housing Booklets and Circulars. The DoE publishes a range of leaflets covering housing issues and gives advice to local authorities about housing issues through circulars. A large public library will have copies of the circulars. Copies of the leaflets including *House Renovation Grants* are available from the Department of Environment, PO Box 151, London E15 2HF. Free on written request.

Shared Ownership, available from the Housing Corporation, 14 Tottenham Court Road, London W1, free.

Index

accommodation
   emergency accommodation 106
   finding alternative accommodation 136-138
   see also: homelessness
accommodation agencies 136
affordable loan 89
aids and adaptation grants
   council tax reductions 53
   valuation band reductions 60
allowances
   attendance allowance 18
   disability living allowance 18
   disability working allowance 18, 19-24
   educational maintenance allowance 18, 25
   family credit 146
   income support 31, 148-150
   mobility allowance 20
annuity mortgage
   see: capital repayment mortgage
appeals
   Child Support Agency 120
   'cohabitation rule' 29
   Consumer Credit Act 84
   council tax 56-58, 60,
     see also: Appendix 4
   excessive mortgage interest 42
   family credit assessments 19
   income support assessments 31, 47-48
   Leasehold Valuation Tribunal 102
   lenders 71, 75
   repair grant decisions 88

   service charges 96-97
   social fund 50
applicable amounts
   disability working allowance 23
   family credit *see:* Threshold
   income support 31
   see also: Appendix 3
arrears 12
   and local authorities 68
   and MIRAS 67/68, 81
   and social services payments 80
   and time order 70, 73, 74, 83
   assistance in negotiating with lender 62-63
   Benefits Agency arrears direct 79, 81
   capital repayments mortgage
   – direct interest payments (IS) 36, 64
   – extending term 64
   – how to negotiate on arrears 64-65
   – reduced capital repayments 81
   reduced mortgage instalments 63-5
   court proceedings 72-74
   endowment mortgage 65
   – changing to repayment mortgage 65
   – negotiating on arrears 66-67, 82-83
   – selling life assurance policy 66
   income support arrears benefit 47
   income support arrears direct 79, 81
   increasing monthly payments 82
   lenders' actions 72-73
   reducing interest payments 63-64
   second mortgages 67-68
   – negotiating 69-70

– refinancing 68
– refinancing on income support 69
service charges 97
  see also: income support, local
    authorities and possession orders
auditing service charges 94, 97

backdating
  council tax rebate 59-60
  family credit claims 17
  income support benefit arrears 47
  income support claims 29, 44
  tax allowances 125
bankruptcy 130
banks
  as lenders 11-12
bathroom fixtures
  council tax disability reduction 53
  interest payments by income
    support 32, 92
  repair grants 87
  valuation band reduction 60
boarders 45
  and council tax 59
borrowing on a mortgage
  see: secured loans
bridging loan 8
  refinancing 68
building insurance 10
building societies
  as lenders 10/11
  Building Societies Association 10,
    Appendix 7
  Building Societies Ombudsman 71,
    162
build up endowment mortgage 5
business
  loans 8
  premises and income support 43

capital
  capital assessment rules 151,
    Appendix 4
  effect of third party payments on
    income support benefit 47

effect on social fund payments 49
for council tax rebates 56, 59
for disability working allowance
  assessment 20
for family credit assessment 17, 132
for income support assessment 28,
  35, 80
mortgage capital 2, 4
capital repayment mortgage 3-4, 6, 11
  reducing payments 63-65
  see also: Appendix 1
capitalising mortgage arrears 81
care and repair grants 87
charge 2, 7-8, 11
  and possession orders 72
  District Land Registry 2, Appendix 7
  Land Charges Registry 2,
    Appendix 7
  registering a charge 108
charities 47, 82
child benefit
  and family credit 18
  and income support 34
  claiming 26
childminding
  and income support 45
  tax allowable costs 19
Child Support Agency 118
children
  ages and family credit 16
  and arrears 80
  and childminding allowance 19
  and council tax 53, 56
  and eviction 137
  and separation 110
  and violence 104-105
  Child Support Agency 118
  childcare costs and benefit 19
  children's earnings and income
    support 34
  dependent when claiming
    disability working allowance 23
  education maintenance allowance 25
  income support allowances 31,
    Appendix 3

INDEX 169

school clothing grants 24
school fares 25
temporarily absent 17
transfer of property order 109
clothing
   school clothing grants 24-25
   social fund 50
cohabitation and income support 29
collective enfranchisement 100-102
commonhold 102
common parts grant 86
community care grants 50
complaints
   against freeholders/agents 96-97
   against lenders 71
Consumer Credit Act 8, 12, 133
   and arrears 70-73
   powers 83-84
co-ownership schemes
   and housing benefit 24
Council of Mortgage Lenders 74, 79, 130
council tax
   absentee owners 55
   and income support 30
   appealing 60
   applicable amounts 56-58, Appendix 4
   backdating claims 59
   benefit and family credit 18
   calculating 56-58
   capital allowances 56
   claiming rebates 59
   death and council tax 52
   definition 52
   disability reduction 53
   discounted people 53
   empty home reduction 52
   evidence of income 56-59
   exceptional benefit 58
   liable residents 54-55
   lone parent premium 57
   non-dependant deductions 57
   paying 55
   reductions 53-54

second adult rebate 53, 58
single person reduction 53
transitional reduction 53-54
valuation bands 52-53, 60
councillors 25
   appealing against council tax 60
   group repair schemes 87
   negotiating on council mortgage 71, 75
   service charge complaints 96
court action
   compulsory enfranchisement 100
   exclusion orders 105
   for leaseholders 96-97
   forfeiture of lease 98
   non-molestation order 104
   order forcing sale 128
   ouster order 104
   personal protection order 105
   possession order 61, 72-74
   time order 70, 73, 83-84
   to change loan agreement 84
   transfer of property order 112
crisis loans 26, 51

damp-proofing 32, 92
default notice 73
   and time order 83
dental treatment
   family credit assistance 16, 25-26
   income support assistance 48
   people on low incomes 26
direct payments
   child support assessment 119
   family credit 15
   income support 36
disabled facilities grant 86
   and council tax 53, 57
   and valuation band 60
disability living allowance
   calculating 23
   claiming 21
disability working allowance 19-24
disasters 26, 51
District Land Registry 2, Appendix 7

district valuer 60
divorce
    and income support 31
    staying in home 108-109
domestic violence 104-105
    and two homes payment 108/109
draught-proofing 90

educational maintenance allowance
    claiming 25
    when calculating family credit 18
elderly peoples' adaptation grants 87
electricity
    income support wiring payments 32, 92
emergencies 51
endowment mortgage 4-6
    build-up endowment 5-6
    changing to repayment 65
    different types 5-6
    guaranteed endowment 5
    housing costs for income support 32
    low-cost endowments 5-6
    managing arrears 65-67
    non-profit endowment 5
    paying interest only 67
    premiums 2
    with profits endowment 5
endowment policies 4, 8-9
equity 2, 83
eviction 74
exclusion order 105

family credit
    annual increases 15
    appealing 19
    backdating 17
    calculating 18
    capital rules 17
    children's rates 15
    claiming 15-16
    direct payments 15
    evidence of income 16
    help with related benefits 25-26

    hours of work 15
    interim payments 15
    overtime effects on 17
    seasonal work 16
    self-employment 14, 16, 19
    shift work 17
    tariff income 17
    threshold 18
    who can claim 15
    when to claim 16
fares
    community care grants 50
    hospital fares 16, 49
    school fares 25
finance companies 12
    new mortgages 68
    on separation 113
first-time buyers
    and valuation bands 60
fixed interest rate mortgages 7
forfeiture of lease 97
    relief against 98
freehold acquisition 98
fuel
    connections help from social fund 50
    council tax reductions 58
    energy efficiency grants 90-91
    income support interest payments 92
funeral costs help 16, 49
furniture
    social fund help 50

gas
    central heating installation and income support 32, 92
    social fund help 50
glasses
    help with costs 16, 25-26
green form scheme 157
group repair schemes 87
guaranteed endowment mortgage 5
guarantor 81, 135
guardian's allowance 19

INDEX

health benefits 16, 25-26, 48-49
heating
    and income support loan payments 32, 92
    council tax reductions 58
    insulation 90-91
    tenants' payments and income support claims 35
HIV 4, 19-24
home improvements 85-102
Home Energy Efficiency Scheme 90
home repairs
    and council tax 60
    grants 85-102
homelessness 106, 111, 127, 138
    homelessness review 140
hospital fares 16, 25, 49
hospital patients and council tax 52
house in spouse's name 105
houses in multiple occupation 86
housing associations 137
    see also: shared ownership
housing benefit 24
    and family credit 18
    and disability working allowance 23

immigrants and benefit claims 14, Appendix 7
improvements 85-102
    and income support 32
    grants 85-86
incapacity benefit
    see: attendance, disability living and disability working allowances
income support
    allowances 31, Appendix 3
    appealing 47-48
    backdating 47
    boarders 45
    business premises 43
    calculating 31, Appendix 3
    capital limits 35
    capital payments income support

    tables Appendix 1
    childminding 45
    claiming 29-30
    council tax benefit 30
    disability adaptation loans 38
    disabled workers 19
    for ground rent 32
    health and education benefits 48-49
    improvement loan interest paid 32, 37
    invalidity benefit 34
    leaseholders' service charges 32
    maintenance payments 34
    direct maintenance payments 36, 79
    mortgage interest payments 31-32, 37
    non-dependants' deductions 41
    rates Appendix 3
    reducing repayment premiums 64
    refinancing on income support 69
    rental income assessment 35
    repair loan interest payments 32, 37
    right to buy service charges 43
    shared ownership costs 40
    sixteen-week rule 40-41
    tenants 45-46
    unapplicable loans 37
    when to claim 29-30
    who can claim 28-29
indemnity insurance 9, 129
insulation grants 90
    and income support 32, 92
insurance companies 11, 61-62
insurance policies 8-10
    and income support 28, 32
intentionally homeless 138
interest 1, 4
    accumulated low-start interest payments by income support 36
    allocation of interest 122
    deferring payments 63
    excessive payments 42
    fixed rate mortgages 7
    income support – 16-week rule 40
    interest only mortgage 6

payments by income support 31-32, 36-37
payments tables Appendix 1
invalidity benefit 34
see also: incapacity benefit

joint homes
and council tax 54
and income support 28, 36, 37
and negative equity 129

Land Charges Registry 2, Appendix 7
Landlord and Tenant Act 1987 10
late claims
council tax rebates 59
for family credit 16
for income support 47
for service charges 96
leaseholds 10
advice on buying freehold 102
buying freehold 98-102
income support for service charges 32-33
major works consultation 95-96
repair/improvement rights 94
service charges 94, 96
Leasehold Reform Act 1993 98-102
Leasehold Valuation Tribunal 101
legal aid
and family credit 16
and possession orders 77
and separation 103
see also: Appendix 6
lenders 2, 10
appeals to 71
arrears action 71-74
banks 11-12
building societies 10-11
finance companies 12
insurance companies 11
local authorities 11
negotiating with
– on arrears 61-63
– on separation 115-116
repossession by 127

types of lender 10-12
life assurance policies 2, 4-6, 11
and income support 28, 32
selling due to arrears 66
treatment for family credit 15
see also: surrender value
loans – changing terms 61-71
local authorities 127
council tax benefit 55
educational maintenance allowance 25
group repair schemes 87
guaranteeing capitalised arrears 81
guaranteeing second mortgage 135
housing 138
housing benefit 24
major works 95
mortgage lender 11
refinancing local authority loan 68
repair grants 85-86
right to buy service charges 94-95
school clothing grants 24-25
school fares 25
temporary accommodations 106
local government ombudsman 71, 96
lodgers
see: boarders
lone parents
and income support 29
council tax premium 57
low-cost endowment mortgage 5, 9
low-start capital repayment mortgage 4, 6-7
and income support accumulated interest payments 36
lump sums
and arrears 79-80, 44
buy out ex-partner 112
repairs and adaptations 85-87
social fund 49
see also: charities

maintenance
and family credit 17
and income support 30, 34

and tax 122-125
major works 95
maladministration
   and arrears 71
   and council tax 60
maternity
   allowance and family credit 19
   needs payment 16, 49
Matrimonial Homes Act 79
Mesher Order 111
milk
   entitlement 25-26, 48
   help with 16
minor works assistance 87
MIRAS 12-13
   and arrears management 67-68
   capitalising 81
   see also: Appendix 1
mobility allowance
   when claiming disability working allowance 20
mortgage
   annuity 3-4
   capital repayment 3-4
   – extending term 64
   – low-start capital repayment 4, 6-7
   see also: Appendix 1
   endowment mortgage 4-6
   – arrears management 65-66
   – build up endowment 5-6
   – changing type 65
   – guaranteed endowment 5
   – low-cost endowment 5-6, 9
   – non-profit endowment 5
   – with profits endowment 5
   indemnity insurance 9
   increasing income for mortgage payments 44-47
   income support arrears payments 79
   interest only mortgage 6
   interest tables Appendix 1
   local authority second mortgage 11
   pension-linked mortgage 6
   protection policy 4
   remortgaging 68-69

   rescue schemes 130
   secured loans 8
   shared ownership 7
   tax relief 12-13
   term 2
   topping up 11
   types of lender 10-12
mortgagee 2
   see: lender
moving home
   and council tax 60
   and income support 32

negative equity 3, 83, 127
new mortgages
   and arrears assistance 66
nominee purchaser 101
non-dependants
   and council tax 57
   and family credit 18
   and income support 41
non-molestation order 104
non-profit mortgage 5

ombudsmen 71, 96
one parent benefit 18
one parent families
   see: lone parents
ouster order 104
outright possession order 3, 74
overtime and family credit 17

paid-up value 65
part-time work 27-51
particulars of claim
   see: possession proceedings
payments 1-2, 9
   by non-entitled spouse 105
pension linked mortgages 6
personal allowances
   and income support 31, Appendix 3
   and tax 126
personal protection order 105
poll tax
   see: council tax

possession proceedings
  adjournment 76-77, 127
  possession order 3, 61, 72-74
  see also: outright possession order
possession warrant 73
premiums
  council tax – lone parent 57
  endowment premium 2
  temporary suspension 65
  income support 31, Appendix 3
prescriptions
  help with cost 16, 25-26, 48
priority need 106, 112, 138
property settlement 104
property transfer 113
protection policy 4, 9
  and income support 34
  claiming arrears 61-62

qualifying tenants 99

rebates
  council tax 24, 53-54, 55-59
  housing benefit 24
  income tax 125
redecoration – social fund loans 51
redeeming mortgage 12
redemption figure 69
reducing mortgage costs 61-71
refinancing 67-68
relationship breakdown 27, 103-126
remortgaging 13, 65, 68-69
removals and social fund loans 51
renovation grants 85-86, 89
rents into mortgages 7
  and housing benefit claims 24
repairs 85-102
  income support interest payments 32
  social fund minor repair grants 50
repayment mortgage 3-4
  see also: arrears, capital repayment mortgage and mortgages
repayments 1-2, Appendix 1, 141
  tables 142

residential care
  community care grants 50
reviews of social fund decisions 50
right to buy 11
  and income support 43
  and service charges 94-95
  see also: local authority

sale of home
  buying share on income support 36
  clearing arrears 71
  when separating 103, 107, 111
savings
  for benefit assessments
  – council tax rebate 56, 59
  – disability working allowance 20
  – income support 28, 35
  – social fund 49-50
school clothing 24
school fares 25
school meals 49
seasonal work 16
section 17 payments 80
secured loans 7-8, 10-12
  and arrears 67-68, 78
  and income support interest payments 32
separation
  and arrears 61-71, 79
  and bankruptcy 130
  divorce 113
  income support 27, 37, 40, 43
  preventing sale of home 107
  property settlements 109
  registering a charge 108
  statement of mortgage account 76
  tax 121-126
  unmarried 113
  with violence 104
service charges 32, 94, 96
shared ownership mortgages 7, 136
  and housing benefit 24
  and income support 28, 42
single parents
  see: lone parents

social fund 49
   cold weather grants 49
   community care grants 50
   entitlement for crisis loans 26
   funeral expenses 49
   maternity expenses 49
   rent in advance 136
   when calculating family credit 18
social services and arrears payments 80
solicitors
   and arrears 63
   and separation 103
   see also: Appendix 6, 156
statutory charge 158
statutory maternity pay 19
statutory sick pay 17
study grant
   see: educational maintenance allowance
summons for arrears 61-62, 73
surrender value 65
suspended possession order 3, 73

tariff income 17
tax 12
   allocation of interest relief 122
   backdating allowances 125
   childminding allowance 19
   collective enfranchisement 100
   maintenance relief 122-125
   rebates 125
   repair loans 91
   when separating 121
   see also: MIRAS
temporary accommodation
   and income support payments 33
   and separation 106
tenants and income support claims 35, 45-46
term 2
   extending capital repayment term 64
threshold 18
time order 70, 83
topping up mortgage 11
   see also: insurance companies
transfer of property when separating 113
wages
   assessment for income support 34
   evidence for council tax rebates 56-59
   evidence when claiming family credit 16
with-profits endowment mortgage 5
women's aid refuges 106

SHAC publications: a selection

Security of Tenure in the Private Rented Sector
Russell Campbell
(edited by John Gallagher)
*was £24.95
reduced to £18.00*
Continuing work done by the Association of Housing Aid, SHAC has taken on the publication of this important guide for lawyers and advisers. An absolutely indispensable aid to all workers in the field, the guide is published in loose-leaf format for easier updating and will find a permanent place in the libraries of all advice agencies, law centres and indeed anywhere where a clear, authoritative guide to housing law and practice is required.

Rights Guide for Home Owners
Paul Moorhouse &
David Thomas   £7.95
The tenth edition is completely revised and updated, and for the first time includes council tax, council tax benefit, leaseholders' rights and the impact of the Child Support Act. Also covers: cutting mortgage costs, repairs and improvements, arrears and avoiding repossession.
ISBN 0 946744 58 0   1994

Housing Rights Guide
Geoffrey Randall   £10.95
The essential guide for all tenants and leaseholders, this guide is now in its fifth edition and has established itself as the leading publication in the field both for the general public and for the generalist adviser.
ISBN 0 948857 40 4   1994

Guide to Council Tax
John Zebedee   £10.50
An essential reference book for administrators and advisers. Covers valuations; who pays; reductions for the disabled; discounts; council tax benefit' transitional reductions; information required from the public; arrears and enforcement; appeals.
ISBN 0 948857 58 7   1993

Guide to Housing Benefit and Council Tax Benefit
Ward & Zebedee   £10.95
Produced jointly by SHAC and the Institute of Housing, this is recognised as the authoritative guide to the subject and is used by advisers and local authorities throughout the country. Updated annually, it is an essential tool for all workers in the field.
ISBN 0 948857 69 2   1994

SPECIAL OFFER
Buy the SHAC *Guide to Council Tax* together with the *Guide to Housing Benefit and Council Tax Benefit* for only £15 – and receive our *Coun cil Tax Update* completely free.

See over for order form

Order form

Title	Price	Copies
Housing Rights Guide	10.95	
Security of Tenure in the Private Rented Sector	18.00	
Rights Guide for Home Owners	7.95	
Guide to Housing Benefit and Council Tax Benefit 1994-95	10.95	
Guide to Council Tax	10.50	
Buying a Home	4.95	
The New Homeless	3.95	
Special offer: Guide to Housing Benefit and Council Tax Benefit *with* Guide to Council Tax 1993-94	15.00	

Cost of publications	
Add post and packing – £1 per item	
TOTAL ENCLOSED	

I enclose a cheque/postal order for £ .... payable to SHAC

Name ....

Address ....

....

.... Postcode .... Telephone ....

Please return this form with your payment to:
**SHAC Publications
Kingsbourne House
229-231 High Holborn, London WC1V 7DA**
Telephone 071-404 7447

Here is my donation to SHAC – London's first independent housing aid centre

Name ....

Address ....

....

.... Postcode ....

Please tick as appropriate:

☐ £1,000   ☐ £500   ☐ £100   ☐ £50

A sum of your choice: £ _____

Send your donation to:
**Clive Landa MBE
SHAC
Kingsbourne House
229-231 High Holborn
London WC1V 7DA**

*Registered as a Charity No 259975
VAT Registration No 240313907*

A CPAG HANDBOOK – new edition

Council Tax Handbook
2nd edition
Martin Ward

CHILD POVERTY ACTION GROUP

The **Council Tax Handbook** is the most widely used practical guide to all aspects of the tax. The second edition is indispensable as it incorporates all that has been learnt after 18 months of the scheme in operation. It covers the position in England, Wales and Scotland, and is completely revised, updated and expanded in the light of legislative changes and practical experience since implementation. New amendments covered include changes regarding discounts, and on exempt properties.

There are full details on: which homes are subject to the tax, valuation, how the tax is worked out and who has to pay, discounts and exemptions, the billing authority's powers to obtain and provide information, tax collection, enforcement and appeals. Fully indexed and cross-referenced to law and regulations.

'Covers all aspects of the tax and its application' – *Financial Times*

'Follows the by now familiar format of other CPAG guides ... will be required by those advising people on how to reduce their council tax bills and anyone who needs to understand the scheme' – *The Adviser*.

November 1994   0 946744 65 3   £8.95

Please send me _____ copies of the **Council Tax Handbook** @ £8.95 each (incl p&p)

I enclose a cheque/PO for £_____ payable to CPAG Ltd

Name _____

Address _____

_____

_____ Postcode _____

Send payment with order to CPAG Ltd, 1-5 Bath Street, London EC1V 9PY

A CPAG HANDBOOK – new edition

Child Support Handbook
2nd edition: 1994/95
Alison Garnham
and Emma Knights

CHILD POVERTY ACTION GROUP

This book is already established as the most widely used guide to all aspects of child support. The 2nd edition is indispensable as it incorporates all that has been learnt from the first year of the scheme in operation.

There is expanded coverage of such issues as the take-on of cases over the transitional period, and CSA procedures for tracing absent parents, making and reviewing assessments, and dealing with paternity disputes. Practical examples – updated to reflect 1994 changes to the formula – are used to illustrate the full range of different family circumstances. There are also tactical hints and arguments for use when seeking review or appeal. The **Child Support Handbook** is fully indexed and cross-referenced to law and regulations.

448 pages   0 946744 61 0   April 1994   £6.95
(£2.45 for benefit claimants – direct from CPAG)

Please send me _____ copies of the **Child Support Handbook** @ £6.95 each (incl p&p)

I enclose a cheque/PO for £_____ payable to CPAG Ltd

Name _____

Address _____

_____

_____ Postcode _____

Send payment with order to CPAG Ltd, 1-5 Bath Street, London EC1V 9PY

A CPAG HANDBOOK

Fuel Rights Handbook
9th edition
Antoinette Hoffland
and Nicholas Nicol

CHILD POVERTY ACTION GROUP

'There has never been a greater need for a definitive guide to fuel rights. It will be no surprise to avid CPAG fans that this is it… CPAG – what would we do without you?' – *The Adviser*

'The presence of the **Fuel Rights Handbook** on an adviser's bookshelf *is* imperative – I can honestly use no other word. You will not be able to say that you are properly resourced without this indispensable publication from the CPAG stable. Like me, you may only use it a few times a year, but that does not undervalue its excellence in any way. Buy this book.' – *Roof*

| 320 pages | 0 946744 57 2 | November 1993 | £7.95 |

Please send me _____ copies of the **Fuel Rights Handbook** @ £7.95 each (incl p&p)

I enclose a cheque/PO for £_____ payable to CPAG Ltd

Name _____

Address _____

_____

_____

_____ Postcode _____

Send payment with order to CPAG Ltd, 1-5 Bath Street, London EC1V 9PY